FINAL DRAFT 1

Series Editor: **Jeanne Lambert**
The New School

David Bohlke
Robyn Brinks Lockwood
Stanford University
Pamela Hartmann

with
Wendy Asplin, University of Washington

CAMBRIDGE
UNIVERSITY PRESS

CAMBRIDGE
UNIVERSITY PRESS

32 Avenue of the Americas, New York, NY 10013-2473, USA

Cambridge University Press is part of the University of Cambridge.

It furthers the University's mission by disseminating knowledge in the pursuit of education, learning and research at the highest international levels of excellence.

www.cambridge.org
Information on this title: www.cambridge.org/9781107495357

© Cambridge University Press 2016

First published 2016

Printed in Dubai by Oriental Press

A catalog record for this publication is available from the British Library.

Cataloging in Publication data is available at the Library of Congress.

ISBN 978-1-107-49535-7 Student's Book Level 1
ISBN 978-1-107-49537-1 Student's Book with Writing Skills Interactive Level 1
ISBN 978-1-107-49538-8 Teacher's Manual Level 1

Additional resources for this publication at www.cambridge.org/finaldraft

Art direction, book design, and photo research: emc design limited
Layout services: emc design limited

CONTENTS

SCOPE AND SEQUENCE

All academic vocabulary words appear on the Academic Word List (AWL) or the General Service List (GSL). ◉ All academic collocations, academic phrases, and common grammar mistakes are based on the Cambridge Academic Corpus.

WRITING SKILLS	GRAMMAR FOR WRITING	AVOIDING PLAGIARISM
Simple and compound sentences Capitalization and punctuation	Simple present	Ways to avoid plagiarism
Writing good topic sentences Titles	Common verb + preposition combinations	Strategies to avoid plagiarism
Complex sentences Avoiding sentence fragments	Pronouns	What is common knowledge?
Transitions of sequential order Adding details	Imperatives	Finding sources
Paragraph unity	Subject relative clauses	Quoting others
Adding details with adjectives and adverbs	*There is* and *There are*	Sharing ideas
Formal vs. informal language Word forms	Superlatives	Using quotations
Avoiding run-on sentences and comma splices	Parallel structure	Creating a "Works Cited" page

TOUR OF A UNIT

ACADEMIC WRITING AND VOCABULARY

Students begin to explore a rhetorical mode and connect it to their everyday lives.

Next, students prepare for their writing by learning corpus-informed academic vocabulary, collocations, and phrases.

ANALYSIS OF TWO WRITING MODELS

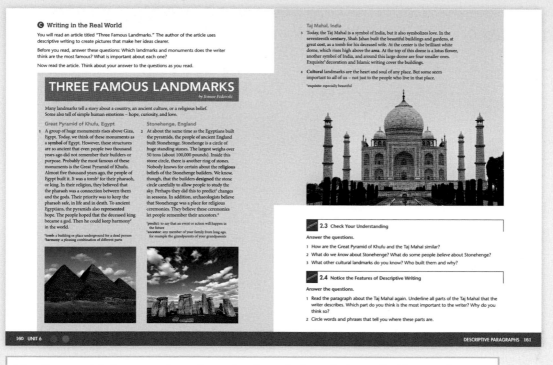

The first model shows students how the rhetorical mode is applied in a real-world setting, helping them recognize that academic writing is all around them.

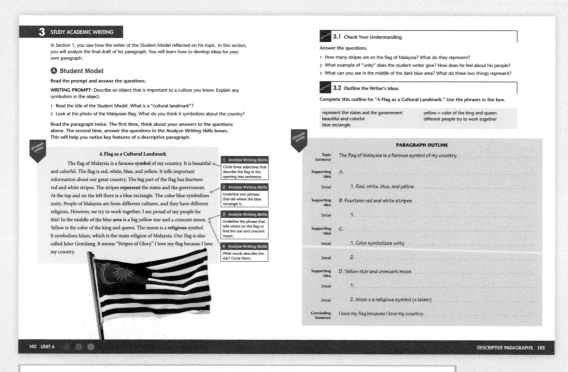

The second model shows a typical assignment from a college writing course. Students analyze this in detail, preparing for their own writing.

4 SHARPEN YOUR SKILLS

Ⓐ Writing Skill 1: Transitions of Sequential Order

Good writers help their readers follow the various steps in the process they are describing. They use certain words and phrases, called **transitions**, that signal the introduction of a new step. These transitions are similar to the ones used for chronological order. After all of these transition words, a comma (,) is required.

TRANSITIONS OF SEQUENTIAL ORDER	
1	A writer often indicates the first step in a process by saying *First* or *First of all*.	***First***, *look at the screen to see where the paper is stuck.*
2	The writer may choose to indicate each step with a number, such as *Second*, *Third*, and *Fourth*. These are used when there are only a few steps in the process.	*First, look at the screen to see where the paper is stuck.* ***Second***, *open the part of the printer where the paper is.* ***Third***, *gently pull the paper from the copier.* ***Fourth***, *close the part of the printer where the paper was.*
3	Another way the writer can indicate each step is by saying *Next*, *Then*, and *After that*. These can be repeated and all mean the same thing.	*First, look at the screen to see where the paper is stuck.* ***Next***, *open the part of the printer where the paper is.* ***Then***, *gently pull the paper from the copier.* ***After that***, *close the part of the printer where the paper was.*
4	The writer can indicate the final step by saying *Finally* or *Lastly*.	***Finally***, *give time for the printer to warm back up.*

4.1 Write Transitions

Complete the paragraph using the transition words below. More than one answer may be possible.

after that	first of all	lastly	next	then

How to Fill a Photocopier

It's very simple to fill a photocopier with paper. _____ (1), find the drawer in the copier that holds the paper. _____ (2), gently pull out the drawer. _____ (3), open a packet of paper and run your thumb along the edges. This helps separate the paper so it does not stick together later. _____ (4), place the paper inside the drawer and make sure it's in place. _____ (5), close the drawer. Now you're ready to copy again with new paper.

> Students develop an extensive skill set, preparing them for every aspect of academic writing.

> Students study specific applications of grammar for the writing task and learn to avoid common mistakes (informed by the Cambridge Learner Corpus).

Avoiding Common Mistakes 👁

Research tells us that these are the most common mistakes that students make when using subject relative clauses in academic writing.

1 Use *who* for people and *that* for things. Do not use *that* for people and *who* for things.
   An academic counselor is a person that helps students plan their courses. (who)
   A scholarship is an award of money who helps a student further his or her education. (that)

2 The verb after a relative pronoun agrees with the noun that the pronoun modifies.
   This is extremely beneficial for students who wants to get a job right away. (want)

3 Do not use a subject pronoun after a relative pronoun.
   A diagnostic test is a test that it assesses a student's current ability.

4 Do not omit a subject relative pronoun.
   This is an advantage for those students already know what they want to do. (who)

4.4 Editing Task

Find and correct four more mistakes in the paragraph below.

A Major

In North America, a major is a specific subject who (which) a student studies while working toward a college degree. Typically between a third and a half of a student's courses are part of his or her major. The other courses are known as core courses. These consist of classes that all students they have to take. Students usually need to choose a major by the end of their second year of study. Students who wants to can also choose two majors. This is called a double major. This is an advantage for students can't decide between two majors. Another option is choosing a major and a minor. A minor is similar to a major. It's also a specific subject area who a student studies, but students need to take fewer classes to achieve a minor. Choosing a major is clearly an important part of the college experience.

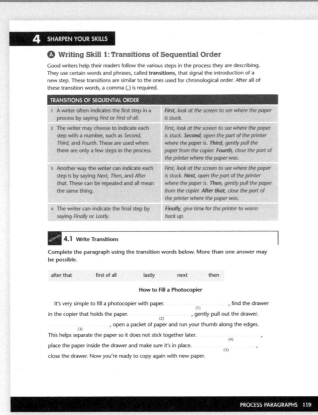

AVOIDING PLAGIARISM AND WRITING YOUR FINAL DRAFT

▶ Avoiding Plagiarism

When you write a college assignment, you should use your own ideas and words.

Q I am worried. I often cannot write my thoughts in English, and I do not want to make a mistake when I write. Sometimes I like to use other people's words. Their words express my ideas. They say them more clearly than I do, but my teacher says I am plagiarizing. I don't understand.

– Roberto

A Dear Roberto,

Do you play soccer? Maybe you do. Do you play like the Argentinian superstar Lionel Messi? You probably don't. However, you still play the game and work towards improving your skills. It is the same in writing. You might find a really good author. You like the author's ideas, but you can't just use his or her words. If you just use someone else's words or ideas, it is wrong. You need to think for yourself and say things in your own words. Your instructors enjoy reading your ideas and helping you become the best writer you can be.

Yours truly,

Professor Wright

STRATEGIES TO AVOID PLAGIARISM

Here are some common thoughts that students have about writing. Think about your last writing assignment. Were any of these true for you?

☐ I can't express my ideas well in English.

☐ I need to get a good grade.

☐ I don't have enough time to do this writing assignment.

Sometimes students plagiarize for the reasons above. On the next page are some strategies to help you avoid plagiarizing for those reasons.

> Students learn to acknowledge others' work and ideas and appropriately incorporate them into their writing.

> Now fully prepared, students write, moving from brainstorming to their final draft.

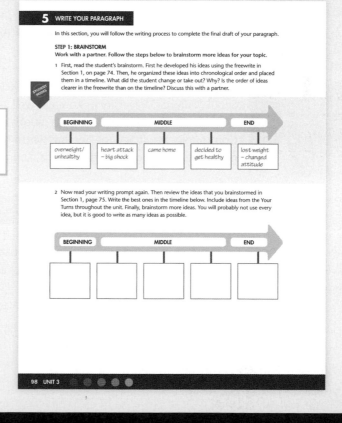

5 WRITE YOUR PARAGRAPH

In this section, you will follow the writing process to complete the final draft of your paragraph.

STEP 1: BRAINSTORM

Work with a partner. Follow the steps below to brainstorm more ideas for your topic.

1 First, read the student's brainstorm. First he developed his ideas using the freewrite in Section 1, on page 74. Then, he organized these ideas into chronological order and placed them in a timeline. What did the student change or take out? Why? Is the order of ideas clearer in the freewrite than on the timeline? Discuss this with a partner.

BEGINNING — MIDDLE — END

| overweight/ unhealthy | heart attack – big shock | came home | decided to get healthy | lost weight – changed attitude |

2 Now read your writing prompt again. Then review the ideas that you brainstormed in Section 1, page 75. Write the best ones in the timeline below. Include ideas from the Your Turns throughout the unit. Finally, brainstorm more ideas. You will probably not use every idea, but it is good to write as many ideas as possible.

BEGINNING — MIDDLE — END

THE TEAM BEHIND *FINAL DRAFT*

SERIES EDITOR

Jeanne Lambert brings 20 years of ESL classroom, teacher training, and materials writing experience to her role as series editor of *Final Draft*. Jeanne has taught at Columbia University, City University of New York (CUNY), and The New School, specializing in academic writing and English for Academic Purposes. While at Columbia University, she taught writing courses in both the American Language Program and for the School of International and Public Affairs. At CUNY, she co-designed a faculty development program to help high school teachers align their ESL reading and writing curriculum with college standards. She has worked as an ESL Methods Practicum instructor and currently teaches academic writing at The New School.

AUTHORS

David Bohlke has been actively involved in ELT since 1987. He has taught in Asia, Africa, and the Middle East and frequently conducts teacher-training sessions around the world. He has served as a writer and series editor of numerous ESL publications.

Robyn Brinks Lockwood teaches at Stanford University's Language Center and is the coordinator for the American Language and Culture summer program. She has authored and edited a wide range of print and digital ELT materials and has presented at numerous national and international conferences.

Pamela Hartmann, who has more than 30 years of experience, taught EFL at Seoul National University in Korea as well as in Greece before settling in Los Angeles, California, where she has taught ESL at colleges and now at Evans Community Adult School. She has written a number of ESL textbooks and has given presentations throughout Asia, Latin America, and the United States.

ACADEMIC WRITING ADVISORY PANEL

The Advisory Panel is comprised of experienced writing instructors who have helped guide the development of this series and have provided invaluable information about the needs of ESL student writers.

Laszlo Arvai, Borough of Manhattan Community College, New York, NY

Leo Kazan, Passaic County Community College, Paterson, NJ

Amy Nunamaker, San Diego State College, San Diego, CA

Amy Renehan, University of Washington, Seattle, WA

Adrianne Thompson, Miami Dade College, Miami, FL

Final Draft was influenced by the opinions and insights of classroom teachers from the following institutions:

UNITED STATES Alabama: Cleburne County High School, Gadsden State Community College, University of Alabama; **Arizona:** Arizona State University, Northern Arizona University, Pima Community College; **Arkansas:** Arkansas State University, University of Arkansas, University of Central Arkansas; **California:** Allan Hancock College, Berkeley High School, California State Polytechnic University, California State University East Bay, California State University Fullerton, California State University Long Beach, California State University Los Angeles, City College of San Francisco, College of San Mateo, De Anza College, Diablo Valley College, East Los Angeles College, El Camino College, The English Center, Evergreen Valley College, Foothill College, Fullerton College, Gavilan College, Glendale Community College, Hollywood High School, Imperial Valley College, Las Positas College, Los Angeles City College, Los Angeles Southwest College, Mendocino College, Mills College, Mission College, Modesto Junior College, Monterey Peninsula College, Palomar College, Pasadena City College, Placer High School, Roybal Learning Center, Sacramento City College, Sacramento State, San Diego Community College District, San Francisco State University, San Jose City College, Santa Ana College, Santa Barbara City College, Santa Monica College, Santa Rosa Junior College, Skyline College, Stanford University, Taft College, University of California Berkeley, University of California Davis, University of California Irvine, University of San Diego, University of San Francisco, University of Southern California, West Valley Community College; **Colorado:** Community College of Aurora, Front Range Community College, Red Rocks Community College, University of Colorado; **Connecticut:** Central Connecticut State University, Enfield High School, Naugatuck Valley Community College, Norwalk Community College, Post University, University of Bridgeport, University of Hartford; **Florida:** Barry University, Florida SouthWestern State College, Florida State University, Hillsborough Community College, Indian River State College, Miami Dade College, Robinson High School, St. Petersburg College, University of Central Florida, University of Florida, University of Miami, University of South Florida; **Georgia:** Augusta State University, Emory University, Georgia Institute of Technology, Georgia Perimeter College, Georgia State University, Interactive College of Technology, Pebblebrook High School, Savannah College of Art and Design, West Hall High School; **Hawaii:** Hawaii Community College, Hawaii Tokai International College, Kapiolani Community College, Mid-Pacific Institute, University of Hawaii; **Idaho:** College of Western Idaho, Northwest Nazarene University; **Illinois:** College of DuPage, College of Lake County, Elgin Community College, English Center USA, Harold Washington College, Harper College, Illinois Institute of Technology, Lake Forest Academy, Moraine Valley Community College, Oakton Community College, Roosevelt University, South Suburban College, Southern Illinois University, Triton College, Truman College, University of Illinois, Waubonsee Community College; **Indiana:** Earlham College, Indiana University, Purdue University; **Iowa:** Divine Word College, Iowa State University, Kirkwood Community College, Mercy College of Health Sciences, University of Northern Iowa; **Kansas:** Donnelly College, Johnson County Community College, Kansas State University, Washburn University; **Kentucky:** Bluegrass Community & Technical College, Georgetown College, Northern Kentucky University, University of Kentucky; **Maryland:** Anne Arundel Community College, Howard Community College, Montgomery College, Johns Hopkins University; **Massachusetts:** Boston University, Mount Ida College, New England Conservatory of Music, North Shore Community College, Phillips Academy, Roxbury Community College, The Winchendon School, Worcester State University; **Michigan:** Central Michigan University, Eastern Michigan University, Grand Rapids Community College, Lansing Community College, Macomb Community College, Michigan State University, Saginaw Valley State University, University of Detroit Mercy, University of Michigan,

Wayne State University, Western Michigan University; **Minnesota:** Century College, Saint Paul College, University of Minnesota, University of St. Thomas; **Mississippi:** Mississippi College, Mississippi State University; **Missouri:** Missouri State University, St. Louis Community College, Saint Louis University, University of Missouri, Webster University; **Nebraska:** Union College, University of Nebraska; **Nevada:** Truckee Meadows Community College, University of Nevada; **New Jersey:** Bergen Community College, The College of New Jersey, Hudson County Community College, Kean University, Linden High School, Mercer County Community College, Passaic County Community College, Rutgers University, Stockton University, Union County College; **New Mexico:** University of New Mexico; **New York:** Alfred State College, Baruch College, Borough of Manhattan Community College, City University of New York, Columbia University, Fashion Institute of Technology, Hofstra University, Hostos Community College, Hunter College, John Jay College of Criminal Justice, Kingsborough Community College, The Knox School, LaGuardia Community College, LIC/LISMA Language Center, Medgar Evers College, New York University, Queens College, Queensborough Community College, Suffolk Community College, Syracuse University, Zoni Language Centers; **North Carolina:** Central Carolina Community College, Central Piedmont Community College, Duke University, Durham Technical Community College, South Piedmont Community College, University of North Carolina, Wake Technical Community College; **North Dakota:** Woodrow Wilson High School; **Ohio:** Columbus State Community College, Cuyahoga Community College, Kent State University, Miami University Middletown, Ohio Northern University, Ohio State University, Sinclair Community College, University of Cincinnati, University of Dayton, Wright State University, Xavier University; **Oklahoma:** University of Oklahoma; **Oregon:** Chemeketa Community College, Clackamas Community College, Lewis & Clark College, Portland Community College, Portland State University, Westview High School; **Pennsylvania:** Pennsylvania State University, University of Pennsylvania, University of Pittsburgh; **Puerto Rico:** Carlos Albizu University, InterAmerican University of Puerto Rico; **Rhode Island:** Johnson & Wales University, Salve Regina University; **South Carolina:** University of South Carolina; **South Dakota:** Black Hills State University; **Tennessee:** Southern Adventist University, University of Tennessee, Vanderbilt University, Williamson Christian College; **Texas:** Austin Community College, Colleyville Heritage High School, Collin College, Dallas Baptist University, El Paso Community College, Houston Community College, Lone Star College, Northwest Vista College, Richland College, San Jacinto College, Stephen F. Austin State University, Tarrant County College, Texas A&M University, University of Houston, University of North Texas, University of Texas, Victoria College, West Brook High School; **Utah:** Brigham Young University, Davis Applied Technology College, Weber State University; **Vermont:** Green Mountain College; **Virginia:** College of William & Mary, Liberty University, Northern Virginia Community College, Tidewater Community College; **Washington:** Bellevue College, EF International Language Centers, Gonzaga University, The IDEAL School, Mount Rainier High School, North Seattle College, Peninsula College, Seattle Central College, Seattle University, Shoreline Community College, South Puget Sound Community College, Tacoma Community College, University of Washington, Whatcom Community College, Wilson High School; **Washington, DC:** George Washington University, Georgetown University; **West Virginia:** West Virginia University; **Wisconsin:** Beloit College, Edgewood College, Gateway Technical College, Kenosha eSchool, Lawrence University, Marquette University, St. Norbert College, University of Wisconsin, Waukesha County Technical College

CANADA British Columbia: Vancouver Island University, VanWest College; **Nova Scotia**: Acadia University; **Ontario**: Centennial College, University of Guelph, York University; **Québec**: Université du Québec

MEXICO Baja California: Universidad de Tijuana

TURKEY Istanbul: Bilgi University, Özyeğin University

1 DEVELOPING IDEAS

TECHNOLOGY: COMMUNICATING IN THE MODERN WORLD

> *"Cell phones are so convenient that they're an inconvenience."*
>
> Haruki Murakami
> (1949–)

About the Author:

Haruki Murakami is a Japanese author of novels and short stories.

Work with a partner. Read the quotation about modern communication. Then answer the questions.

1 *Convenient* means helpful or easy. In what ways are cell phones convenient?

2 In what ways are cell phones sometimes inconvenient?

3 Do any types of technology make communication more difficult?

Ⓐ Connect to Academic Writing

In this unit, you will learn skills to help you develop your ideas in your writing. For example, you will learn how to give reasons, give examples, and provide further information with explanations. These are skills you already use in your daily life. For example, you might give a reason for being late to class to your instructor. You might give a friend examples of apps that you find useful in your studies. You might explain to your parents some of the new and interesting things you are learning in class.

Ⓑ Reflect on the Topic

In this section, you will look at a writing prompt and reflect on it. Throughout the unit, you will develop ideas about this prompt. You will use these ideas to practice skills that are necessary to write your paragraph.

The writing prompt below was used for the Student Model paragraph on page 20. The student reflected on the topic and used a cluster diagram to brainstorm ways people use technology to socialize.

STUDENT MODEL

WRITING PROMPT: People are increasingly using technology to socialize. How do people of your age use technology to socialize? Include at least three examples.

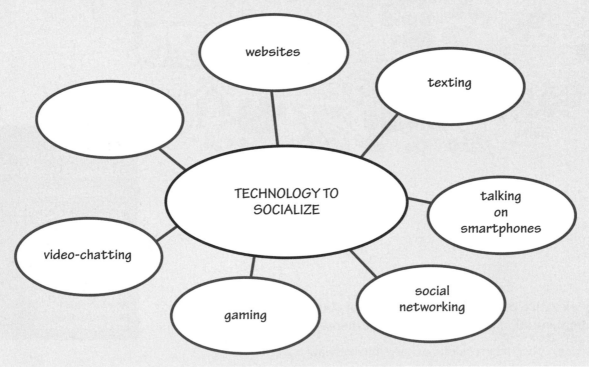

ACTIVITY
1.1 Notice

Tell your partner about one more example you could write about. Then add it to the cluster diagram. Share your ideas with the class.

1.2 Apply It to Your Writing

Read the prompt and follow the directions below.

WRITING PROMPT: Technology is increasingly being used by all age groups. How does one of the age groups listed below use technology?

Children (2–8 years old)   Pre-teens (9–12 years old)
Teenagers (13–19 years old)   Young adults (20–35 years old)
Adults (36–59 years old)   Older adults (60+ years old)

1 Choose one of the age groups. Write it in the center circle of the cluster diagram below.

2 Think about all the ways this age group uses technology. Write those ways in the other circles.

3 Compare cluster diagrams with a partner.

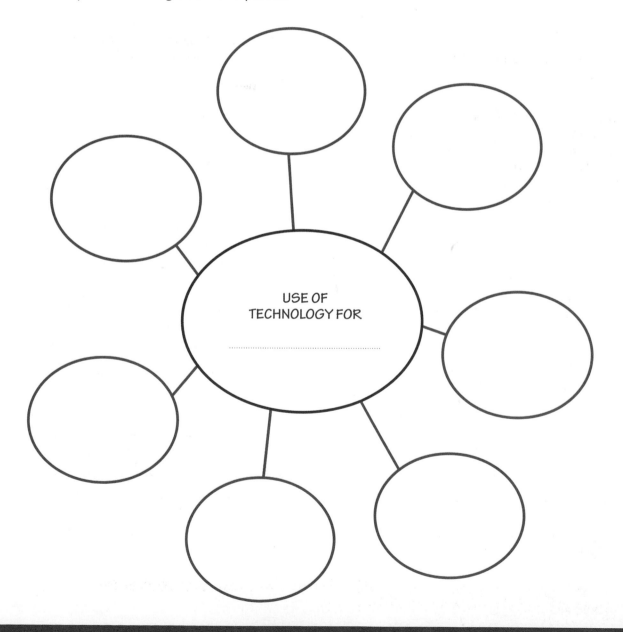

USE OF
TECHNOLOGY FOR

_____

In this section, you will learn academic language that you can use in your paragraph. You will also notice how a professional writer uses this language.

Ⓐ Academic Vocabulary

The words below appear throughout the unit. They are from the Academic Word List or the General Service List. Using these words in your writing will make your ideas clearer and your writing more academic.

contact (v)	exchange (v)	option (n)	trend (n)
essential (adj)	inform (v)	technology (n)	use (v)

 2.1 Focus on Meaning

A Work with a partner. Match the words in bold to their meanings. Write the letters.

.... 1 I get text messages from my phone provider. These messages **inform** me of special offers on new phones.

    a to do something with an object or machine to complete a task

.... 2 People of all ages **use** electronic devices in their daily lives. In the United States, almost 50% of children have cell phones by the age of 10.

    b to give knowledge to someone

.... 3 Modern **technology**, such as smartphones and email, makes it very easy for people to stay in touch.

    c equipment or systems, especially those that have to do with computers and modern science

.... 4 People have more than one **option** for accessing the Internet. They can use a smartphone, a tablet, a laptop, or even a TV.

    d one thing that can be chosen from many possibilities

B Read the paragraph and guess the meaning of the words in bold. Then circle the letter of the correct definition for each word.

Electronic Business Cards

Electronic business cards are a good way to connect professionally. Business cards are an **essential** part of business culture. Businesspeople often **exchange** them when they meet for the first time. The information on a business card allows someone to **contact** another person easily. Printed business cards are still popular, but there is a recent **trend** toward electronic business cards. For example, many businesspeople add their electronic business card at the end of an email. In conclusion, electronic business cards help connect to other people.

1 **Essential** means

   a strange or foreign.   b very important or necessary.

2 To **exchange** means

   a to hide or keep out of view.   b to give and receive the same thing in return.

3 To **contact** means

   a to communicate or get in touch
      with someone.   b to find out something you did not
                                          know before.

4 A **trend** is

   a something that is rarely done anymore.   b the general ways something is changing.

B Academic Collocations

Collocations are words that are frequently used together. Research tells us that the academic vocabulary in Part A is commonly used in the collocations in bold below.

 2.2 Focus on Meaning

Work with a partner. Read the sentences. Decide the meaning of the collocations in bold and circle the correct definitions.

1 Many teachers today **use technology**, such as smartboards and classroom management systems, in their classrooms.

   a use electronic equipment to
      solve problems   b use electronic equipment to
                                     create problems

2 Teachers often allow students to bring smartphones to class. Usually, though, students are not allowed to **exchange messages** on their smartphones during class.

   a read information about someone   b send and receive information with someone

3 Some teachers still accept handwritten homework assignments. The **best option**, though, is for students to type assignments.

   a the only choice   b the number one choice

4 There is a **general trend** toward teachers using more technology in their classrooms. New software allows teachers to manage, track, and deliver educational content online.

   a reasons why something is staying
      the same   b overall way something is developing

5 For many teachers, a textbook, a whiteboard, and a computer are **essential tools** needed to teach students.

   a things that are necessary   b things that are not very useful

C Writing in the Real World

You will read an article titled "How We Use Our Cell Phones." The author of the article develops his ideas so his reader can understand them.

Before you read, answer this question: What do you think are the three most popular uses for cell phones?

Now read the article. Think about your answer to the question as you read.

HOW WE USE OUR CELL PHONES

By Jorge Navarro

1 The cell phone is an **essential** tool for many people. We use it to communicate, to **inform**, to share, and to entertain. According to a survey by the Pew Research Center, 85% of American adults now own a cell phone. The survey also shows some interesting information about how they use their phones. The top five uses for cell phones – besides talking to others – are taking pictures, texting, accessing the Internet, emailing, and recording video.

2 The most popular cell phone activity is taking pictures. Among all cell phone users, 82% **use** their phone to take photos. There is little difference between males and females. For instance, 82% of men and 81% of women take pictures with their phones. Perhaps unsurprisingly, young adults are the most likely to take pictures. Ninety-four percent of those under 29 take pictures with their cell phones, compared to just 44% of those aged 65 and over.

3   The second most popular cell phone activity is texting. A few years ago, 58% of people texted with their phones, but the number today is 80%. Large numbers of users send and receive texts, with the exception of older Americans. Among users 18–29 years of age, texting is nearly universal.[1]

4   Fifty-six percent of cell phone owners access the Internet with their phone, making it the third most common activity. The gap[2] between young and older users is high: 77% of those under 30 access the Internet with their phones versus just 13% of those 65 and older. There is also a large difference according to income. Because it can sometimes be expensive to get online, those who earn more than $75,000 per year are much more likely to access the Internet than those who earn less than $30,000.

5   The fourth most common activity is emailing. Half of users **contact** others via[3] email on their devices. As with other activities, younger users are much more likely to use cell phones to **exchange** messages using email.

[1] **universal**: experienced by everyone
[2] **gap**: difference
[3] **via**: by means of

6   Recording videos is the fifth most popular activity. Forty-four percent of users now make videos with their phones, up from just 18% a few years ago. Seven in 10 young adults record videos with their phones, compared to just 9% of older adults. Younger users are more likely to be comfortable with using this **technology** in their daily lives.

7   How will people use their cell phones in the future? What **options** will cell phones offer that we have not even thought of yet? What general **trends** can we predict? It's anyone's guess!

 2.3 Check Your Understanding

Answer the questions.

1 After "talking," what do most Americans use cell phones for?

2 Which statistic about cell phone use surprised you? Explain your answer.

3 How do your cell phone habits compare to those mentioned in the survey?

 2.4 Notice the Writing

Answer the questions.

1 Read the first paragraph again. Underline the sentence that includes an explanation of why a cell phone is an essential tool.

2 Read the second paragraph again. Underline the two-word phrase that signals an example.

3 Read the fourth paragraph again. Underline the word that signals a reason.

In Section 1, you saw how the writer of the Student Model reflected on her topic. In this section, you will analyze the final draft of her paragraph. You will learn how to develop ideas for your own paragraph.

Ⓐ Student Model

Read the prompt and answer the questions.

WRITING PROMPT: People are increasingly using technology to socialize. How do people of your generation use technology to socialize? Include at least three examples.

1 What are some ways people use technology to socialize?

2 What ways do you think the writer – a young adult – will mention?

Read the paragraph twice. The first time, think about your answers to the questions above. The second time, answer the questions in the Analyze Writing Skills boxes. This will help you notice the key features of a paragraph.

How College Students Use Technology to Socialize

People of my generation **use technology** to socialize in different ways. Nearly everyone I know has a digital device such as a cell phone, tablet, or laptop. College students have several **options** for how they socialize. For many students, texting is the best option for **contacting** friends. People like texting since it's fast and easy. College students are also big users of social media, and this is a great way to socialize with a larger group of people. Interestingly, some students also use social media to communicate with classmates outside of class. They often start discussions about interesting topics that come up in class. Teachers sometimes join in, too. They use these to **inform** students of class updates, such as reminders about homework and quizzes. Finally, video-chatting is also very popular for communicating with families. This is because some people do not live near their families. For example, my family lives eight hours away, so we video-chat every Saturday. Using cell phones, tablets, and laptops is clearly **essential** for socializing for my generation.

1 Analyze Writing Skills

Find a sentence that contains the names of three devices. What punctuation (a period? a comma? a dash?) does the writer use to separate them? Circle them. Underline any capital letters in the sentence.

2 Analyze Writing Skills

Find and circle a word that signals a reason. Underline the reason.

3 Analyze Writing Skills

Find and circle an example of two complete sentences joined by *and*.

4 Analyze Writing Skills

Find and circle a phrase that signals a personal example. Underline the example.

3.1 **Check Your Understanding**

Answer the questions.

1 What three ways of socializing does the writer discuss?

2 According to the writer, what is a good way to socialize with people far away?

3 How do you think the writer might contact several friends that she wants to discuss a class presentation with?

Complete the outline for "How College Students Use Technology to Socialize." Use the phrases in the box.

fast and easy	social media	video-chatting
good for individual friends	some families live far away	good for large groups of people

STUDENT MODEL

PARAGRAPH OUTLINE

First Sentence People of my generation use technology to socialize in different ways.

1st Idea A. Texting

Explanation 1.

Reason 2.

2nd Idea B.

Explanation 1.

3rd Idea C.

Explanation 1. Good for families

Reason 2.

Example 3. Writer's family lives eight hours away

Last Sentence Using cell phones, tablets, and laptops is clearly essential for socializing for my generation.

B Developing Ideas

Good writers develop their ideas so their writing is easily understood and interesting to read. A well-developed paragraph includes **examples**, **reasons**, and **explanations** of the writer's ideas. Read the two paragraphs below. Which paragraph has ideas that are well developed?

Paragraph 1

Why Technology Is Essential for Today's Student

Students today cannot imagine academic life without technology. A digital device is an essential tool for most of my college friends. Many bring their digital devices into class. Students also use their devices to complete assignments. Some teachers in my college only accept assignments prepared in this way, so it's very important for students to be comfortable using technology.

Paragraph 2

Why Technology Is Essential for Today's Student

Students today cannot imagine academic life without technology. A digital device such as a cell phone, tablet, or laptop is an essential tool for most of my college friends. In fact, most students use some sort of digital device to get updated information on their classes from their teachers. Many bring their device into class, since they use it to take notes, record lectures, or even take photos of their professor's slides. This saves time and allows them to share their notes with others after class. Students also use their devices to complete assignments. These assignments consist of online homework that teachers regularly assign. Some teachers only accept assignments prepared in this way, so it's very important for students to be comfortable using technology. In conclusion, technology is very important for students today.

It is clear that paragraph 2 is better. Why? It's because the writer has included examples, reasons, and explanations in her writing. This additional information makes us think about our knowledge of the topic: What are our experiences? Do we agree or disagree with the writer?

 3.3 Notice

Underline the sentences in paragraph 2 above where the writer uses examples, reasons, and explanations.

EXAMPLES

One way to develop ideas is through **examples**. Certain phrases can signal examples.
For example and *For instance* are typically used at the beginning of sentences.

> *People use cell phones for more than phone calls.* **For example,** / **For instance,** *a recent survey found that 82% of American adults use them to take photos.*

Such as is usually followed by nouns, verbs, or other short examples. A sentence generally does not follow *such as*.

> NOUN   NOUN   NOUN
>
> *Digital devices* **such as** *cell phones, tablets, and laptops are an essential part of college life.*

Note that writers can give examples without using signal words.

> *Older people are becoming more comfortable with technology. This is certainly true with my grandmother. She likes to show her friends photos on her cell phone.*

 3.4 Notice

Look back at the Student Model on page 20. What example did you underline? Find and write another sentence in the text that includes an example.

3.5 Write Examples

Complete these sentences with your own examples.

1 There are many ways that smartphones can be useful during an emergency. For example, ...

2 A natural disaster such as ....
   can cause huge damage. An early-warning communication system is essential in order to save lives.

3 It is frustrating to not get help when you need it. For instance, ...

4 There are important phone numbers you should remember in case you need help.

   For example, ...

 3.6 Apply It to Your Writing

Work with a partner. Go to the ideas you wrote in Section 1 on page 14. Look at your ideas and find places to add examples. Note your examples below.

....

....

....

....

REASONS

Another way to develop ideas is through **reasons**. The words *because* and *since* are commonly used to explain reasons. They can begin a sentence. *Because* is used more often than *since*.

> *Many people prefer cell phones **since** they are cheaper than laptop computers.*

> *Since they are cheaper than laptop computers, many people prefer using cell phones.*

 3.7 Notice

Circle the best word to complete each sentence.

1 *Since* is **more / less** commonly used than *because*.

2 The word *since* **can / cannot** begin a sentence.

3 The word *because* **is / isn't** necessary before a reason.

3.8 Complete Reasons

Complete the sentences using the phrases (a–e) below. Write the letters.

a she wanted to share her news immediately

b many people are busy

c these sources can be more entertaining

d they can get more up-to-date news online

e online news sites have comment boxes

1 Many people do not read paper newspapers today because ....

2 Since ...., it's faster for them to check news headlines online.

3 Because ...., anyone can post their own opinion about the news.

4 Because ...., she decided to post it on her social networking page.

5 Many people get their news from blogs because ....

 3.9 Write Ideas

Complete the sentences with your own ideas.

1 The best website to get the latest news is .... because ....

....

2 .... is a popular social networking site because ....

....

3 Because ...., I sometimes only check news about ....

....

4 I never share news about .... with other people online because ....

....

5 Since ...., the best digital device to buy now is ....

....

 3.10 Apply It to Your Writing

Work with a partner. Go to the ideas you wrote in Section 1 on page 14.
Choose one idea and write a reason that supports that idea.

....

....

....

EXPLANATIONS

Another way to develop ideas is through **explanations**. In some cases, a writer might explain a difficult or unfamiliar word or concept. At other times, explanations are simply additional details that help the writer describe or elaborate.

Explanations often answer the questions *How?* or *In what way?* They may include an explanation of how something came to be, how something works, or how things relate to one another.

Read the sentences below. Notice how the second sentence gives more information about the first sentence.

> *In some ways, technology has made people poor communicators. Some people do not listen well because they are always looking at their phones.* (The second sentence explains why they are poor communicators.)

> *Some people think that technology lets people hide behind a "technology wall." This means that people prefer to communicate by texting instead of speaking face to face.* (The second sentence explains what the writer means by "technology wall.")

 3.11 Notice the Writing

Look back at the Student Model on page 20. Check (✓) the ideas that are explained.

☐ 1 how students contact individual friends

☐ 2 the name of a popular app for socializing

☐ 3 what students use email for

☐ 4 how teachers use social media

Complete the paragraph by circling the best explanation.

Is Technology Damaging Our Communications Skills?

Too much technology is damaging our communication skills for several reasons. First, **no one talks to one another anymore. / everybody loves technology, especially young people**. For example, I went to a party last week. Most people were on their smartphones. (1) One person was sending a text. Another person was reading an email. Second, you can now talk to one person while at the same time texting with someone else. In the past, this was considered rude, but not anymore. **No one likes to be around rude people. / Nowadays, people accept this kind of behavior**. Third, communication skills are worse with technology. (2) People say more negative things these days. **It is easy to write negative comments when we cannot see someone. / There are more negative messages on blogs than on social media sites**. Lastly, I think we are also losing our ability to have real conversations. **Some people (3) have many friends online. / We often just send quick messages online**. We have fewer face-to-face conversations. For these reasons, many people believe that technology is damaging (4) our essential communication skills.

A Work with a partner. Use your own ideas to complete the paragraph with a reason, an explanation, and an example.

More Sales with Social Media

Small businesses can use social media to get more customers. One type of business that shows that social media can increase sales is food trucks. There is a food truck near where I work called "Ben's Burgers." People stand in line, order their food, and eat it – often standing up. It does not cost a lot to run a food truck because ....

.... (a reason).

To attract new customers, "Ben's Burgers" has a social media page. They advertise special deals. For example, they offer discounts, have special sales, or advertise different events to get more customers. A food truck is like a moving restaurant. In other words,

....

.... (an explanation). This is useful because they can go wherever there's a crowd. For example, ...
....

(an example). "Ben's Burgers" tweets its location to let customers know where it is. It's a food truck that is doing well because of social media.

B Exchange your work with another pair. Do you have similar reasons, explanations, and examples?

3.14 Apply It to Your Writing

YOUR TURN

Work with a partner. Go to the ideas you wrote in Section 1 on page 15. Look at your ideas. Choose one idea and write one or two sentences to explain it.

....

....

....

....

Ⓐ Writing Skill 1: Simple and Compound Sentences

Good writers use a variety of sentences in their writing to keep the reader's attention. It's important for writers to understand different sentence types so they can use a mix of sentences.

The most basic type of sentence is the **simple sentence**. A simple sentence is an independent clause. It contains a complete thought. Using only simple sentences can produce writing that does not flow well.

SIMPLE SENTENCES

1 A simple sentence contains a **subject** and **verb**.

> SUBJECT VERB
> *My computer crashed*.

2 A simple sentence can also contain an **object**, a **prepositional phrase**, or both.

> OBJECT
> *Businesspeople exchange business cards.*
> PREPOSITIONAL PHRASE
> *Food trucks often tweet in the morning*.
> OBJECT PREPOSITIONAL PHRASE
> *Many teachers use technology in the classroom*.

3 A simple sentence can contain a **compound subject**, **compound verb**, or **compound object**. However, it is still a simple sentence because it contains one complete thought.

> COMPOUND SUBJECT
> *Men and women take photos in equal numbers.*
> COMPOUND VERB
> *Many people text and email each other every day.*
> COMPOUND OBJECT
> *Young people like to take photos and videos*.

ACTIVITY **4.1** Complete Sentences

A Rearrange the words to write simple sentences.

1 I / on my Facebook page / post messages

....

....

2 pizza and burgers / sells / the food truck

....

....

3 write / Dani and Steve / in the evening / a blog

....

....

B Add labels to your sentences above. Write *subject, verb, object, prepositional phrase,* *compound subject,* **and** *compound object.*

Another type of sentence is the **compound sentence**. A compound sentence contains two independent clauses.

COMPOUND SENTENCES	
1 Compound sentences contain a **coordinating conjunction**. A coordinating conjunction links two complete thoughts.	*I text my friends every morning, **and** we speak every evening.*
2 The choice of conjunction can change the meaning of the sentence. *And* adds information. *But* shows contrast. *Or* gives a choice. *So* shows a consequence.	*I text my friends every morning, **but** I prefer talking to them in person.* *I text my friends every morning, **or** I call and speak to them directly.* *I text my friends every morning, **so** I always know what they are doing.*

 4.2 Combine Sentences

Join the two simple sentences to create one compound sentence. Use the best coordinating conjunction in parentheses.

1 It's easy to use Facebook. Even people uncomfortable with technology use it. (so / or)

....

....

....

2 Jim has not joined Facebook. His wife does not think he'll ever join. (and / or)

....

....

....

3 You can "like" people on Facebook. You may choose to follow people. (or / so)

....

....

....

4 Many people still use Facebook. Some people think it will decrease in popularity. (but / so)

....

....

....

B Writing Skill 2: Capitalization and Punctuation

Writers follow certain rules of **capitalization** and **punctuation** when writing.

CAPITALIZATION RULES	
1 Always **capitalize the pronoun** *I*. (Writers do not use this pronoun frequently in academic writing.)	*I check my messages every morning.*
2 Begin each word of a new sentence with a **capital letter**.	*Texting is popular among my friends.* *Emailing is not so popular.*
3 **Capitalize proper nouns**, such as the names of people, places, days of the week, months, holidays, languages, cities, and countries.	*Ian is from **Manchester, England.*** *He moved to **Berlin** last **August.*** *He speaks **German** well.*
4 Do not capitalize **common nouns**. Common nouns are general names of people, places, and things.	*Ian is from a large **city.*** *He has never lived in a foreign **country.*** *He speaks two **languages.***
5 Do not capitalize **seasons**.	*The seasons are **spring, summer, fall,** and **winter.***
6 Do not capitalize **directions**.	*Drive east for a kilometer and then turn **north.***

 4.3 Understand Capitalization

Correct the capitalization errors in the paragraph. There are seven mistakes.

Calling from the Top of the Earth

These days it's easy to keep in touch from the top of Mount Everest. In the past, it was hard to communicate from remote places. Edmund hillary, the first person to reach the top of everest, had to use heavy radio equipment to make calls. Now, both china and Nepal have cell phone networks there, so people can use a cell phone. The use of GPS technology also makes things easier because climbers now know exactly where they are on the mountain. It's also easier for rescuers to find climbers who may need help. For instance, helicopters from areas South of the mountain, or from the City of kathmandu to the west, can quickly go in to rescue climbers during an emergency. Devices such as smartphones also help climbers get current information. It's difficult to predict the weather on Everest during the Summer climbing season, but with a smartphone, climbers can get up-to-date weather forecasts. They can also send emails or post updates about their climb. The top of the world does not seem too distant these days.

PUNCTUATION RULES

1 Always end sentences with a period (.), a question mark (?), or an exclamation point (!). Do not end a sentence with a comma (,).	*Social media can attract new customers.* *How can we use technology to socialize?* *Be careful!*
2 Use commas in a list of three or more words, phrases, and clauses.	*One person may be **sending a text**, another may be **commenting on a blog**, and another may be **reading an email**.*
3 Use commas before coordinating conjunctions (*and, but, or, so*) in compound sentences.	*Printed business cards are still popular, **but** there is a recent trend toward electronic business cards.*
4 Use a comma after phrases such as *for example* and *for instance*.	*There is little difference between males and females. **For instance**, 82% of men and 81% of women take pictures with their phones.*

4.4 Correct Punctuation Mistakes

Add the correct punctuation to these sentences.

1 A British climber named Daniel Hughes became famous in 2013

2 He was the first person to use his smartphone to make a video call from Mount Everest

3 Did he call his grandmother his mother or his friends

4 He called the BBC news organization and they interviewed him

5 Nepal was in the news but the government of Nepal was not happy about it

6 Hughes did not have permission to broadcast so the call is considered illegal

7 The government said that Hughes would be punished for the act

8 For example he could face a 10-year ban from climbing Everest

C Grammar for Writing: Simple Present

The **simple present** is one of the most common tenses in English. Study these uses:

SIMPLE PRESENT	
1 Use the simple present to describe facts and general truths.	*Young people **text** more than older people.* *Both China and Nepal **have** networks on Mount Everest.*
2 It is also used to describe habits and repeated actions.	*Most people **use** cell phones to take photos.* *Large numbers of cell phone users **send** and **receive** texts every day.*
3 It is often used with adverbs of frequency (*always, often, sometimes, never*) and expressions of frequency (*every day, once a week*).	*Students **often start** discussions about interesting topics that come up in class.* *Teachers **sometimes join** the discussions, too.* *I **video-chat** with my family **every Saturday**.*
4 It is also used with stative (non-active) verbs such as *like, hope, have, wish, know, understand, belong, prefer, believe,* and *want*.	*I do not **understand** this message.* *Who **does** that laptop **belong** to?* *How **do** you **prefer** to communicate?*

 4.5 Identify Form

Circle the correct statement(s) about each sentence.

1 I prefer texting to emailing.

   a Is a fact / general truth

   b Is a habit / repeated action

   c Uses a stative verb

2 Teachers seldom allow students to exchange text messages during class.

   a Is a fact / general truth

   b Uses an adverb or expression of frequency

   c Uses a stative verb

3 Fifty-six percent of cell phone owners access the Internet with their phone.

   a Is a fact / general truth

   b Is a habit / repeated action

   c Uses a stative verb

4 At a food truck people stand in line, order their food, and eat it.

   a Is a habit / repeated action

   b Uses an adverb or expression of frequency

   c Uses a stative verb

Complete the sentences with the correct form of the simple present tense.

1 Some people today *do not trust* .... (not / trust) the traditional news media.

2 Citizen journalism .... (refer) to the reporting of news events by everyday people.

3 It often .... (let) people hear two sides of an issue.

4 A citizen journalist .... (not / have) a degree in journalism.

5 Technology .... (play) a big part in citizen journalism.

6 Citizen journalists usually .... (publish) online by using a blog or community website.

7 Certain types of citizen journalism .... (act) as a check on regular news reporting.

8 Some people .... (feel) that citizen journalism is a threat to traditional journalism.

Avoiding Common Mistakes

Research tells us that these are the most common mistakes that students make when using the simple present tense in academic writing.

1 Use the simple present with stative verbs.

      hope
I ~~am hoping~~ to upgrade my phone soon.

2 Use the correct form of *do* with singular and plural subjects.

       do
Young people ~~does~~ not send many emails.

3 Do not use *sometimes* after *not*.

      sometimes
My mother does not ~~sometimes~~ answer my texts. She calls me instead.

 4.7 Editing Task

Find and correct four more mistakes in the paragraph below.

A Job That Uses Technology

                        uses
My uncle is a taxi driver, and he ~~is using~~ technology every day in this job. He has a smartphone. The main taxi office sends him text messages that tell him where to pick up passengers. His family and friends calls him regularly, too. He also has a two-way radio, but he don't use it very much. The main piece of technology my uncle uses is a GPS. My uncle does not sometimes know places in our city, so the GPS technology is very useful. The newest technology in my uncle's taxi is an information tablet for passengers. Passengers can check their route and watch the news. They can even pay for their fare using a credit card. I'm thinking my uncle's job has become easier with the latest technology.

D Avoiding Plagiarism

In North America, people have very strong opinions about plagiarism.

My instructor warned us about plagiarizing other writers' ideas. I know students get in trouble for plagiarizing, but what is plagiarism? Why is it so important in North America?

– Thiago

Dear Thiago,

When you copy someone's exact words or ideas, you are plagiarizing. In some cultures, it is OK to do that. In North America, however, a person's words and ideas are like property. They belong to that person. You can use them, but you must always say where you found them and name the original writer.

Yours truly,

Professor Wright

WAYS TO AVOID PLAGIARISM

Plagiarizing on homework or tests is not acceptable. The consequences are very serious. Read your school's academic integrity policy and make sure you understand it.

Let's look at some ideas that will help you avoid plagiarizing.

DO:	DON'T:
• Use your own words and ideas.	• Do not copy and paste sentences or paragraphs from the Internet.
• Say where you found your information.	• Do not copy exact words from a book or magazine.

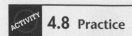 **4.8** Practice

Read the paragraph from an original text. Then read the two paragraphs Students A and B wrote. Student B's writing shows signs of plagiarism. Work with a partner. Underline the phrases that are plagiarized. Discuss the ways Student A avoided plagiarizing.

Psychologist Sherry Turkle studies how technology affects people. In her studies, she found that technology, like text messages and email on a smartphone, changes our social behavior. Now, it's common to talk to someone while texting someone else. In the past, this was considered rude. Today, it's normal. Turkle insists we are losing our ability to have real conversations.

Student A:

Is technology changing the way we behave with people? Sherry Turkle, a psychologist, believes that. For example, nowadays we communicate by text and email to two different people at one time. This is different from the past. She thinks we can't have real conversations now.

Student B:

Technology can change our social behavior. For example, sometimes we talk to someone and text someone else at the same time. In the past, this was rude. Now, we are losing our ability to have real conversations.

In this section, you will follow the **writing process** to complete the final draft of your paragraph. The writing process helps writers think about, organize, and write their ideas.

STEP 1: BRAINSTORM

Work with a partner. Follow the steps below to brainstorm more ideas for your topic.

1 First, read the student's brainstorm. She wrote many ideas from the cluster diagram she used to reflect on her topic in Section 1 on page 14. Finally, she deleted ideas that she thought would not work in her paragraph.

STUDENT MODEL

WRITING PROMPT: People are increasingly using technology to socialize. How do people of your age use technology to socialize? Include at least three examples.

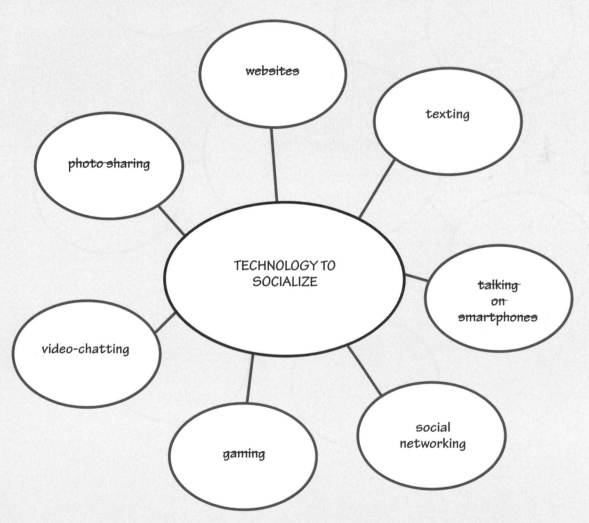

2 Now read your writing prompt again. Then review the ideas that you brainstormed in Section 1 on page 15. Write the best ones in the cluster diagram below. Include ideas from the Your Turns throughout the unit. Finally, brainstorm more ideas. You will probably not use every idea, but it is good to write as many ideas as possible.

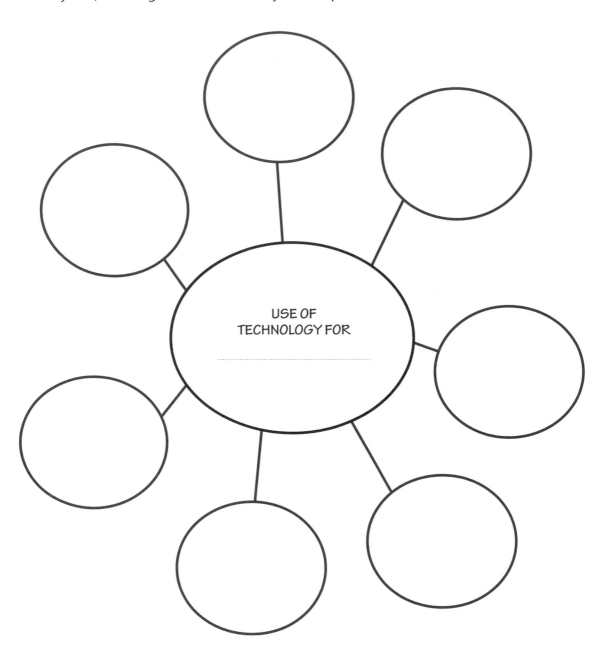

USE OF
TECHNOLOGY FOR

STEP 2: MAKE AN OUTLINE

Making an outline helps you organize ideas. Complete the outline below with ideas for your paragraph from Step 1 on page 40.

PARAGRAPH OUTLINE

First Sentence	
1st Idea	A.
Explanation	1.
Reason	2.
Example	3.
2nd Idea	B.
Explanation	1.
Reason	2.
Example	3.
3rd Idea	C.
Explanation	1.
Reason	2.
Example	3.
Last Sentence	

STEP 3: WRITE YOUR FIRST DRAFT

Now it's time to write your first draft. Here are some suggestions on how to get started.

1 Use your outline and the sentences you wrote in the Your Turns and in Step 2 on page 41.

2 Focus on making your ideas as clear as possible.

3 Add a title.

After you finish, read your paragraph and check for basic errors.

1 Check that all sentences have subjects and verbs.

2 Go through and look at every comma. Is it correct? Should it be a period?

3 Check that you have used a comma after adverb clauses when they start a sentence.

4 Make sure your first sentence and your explanations, reasons, and examples are clear.

STEP 4: WRITE YOUR FINAL DRAFT

1 After you receive feedback on your first draft, review it carefully. Fix any errors.

2 Make a note of errors that were most frequent (misspellings, using commas instead of periods, missing verbs). Try to avoid them as you write.

3 Review the Academic Vocabulary and Academic Collocations from this unit. Are there any that you can add to your paragraph?

4 Turn to page 237 and use the Self-Editing Review to check your work one more time.

5 Write your final draft and hand it in.

2 INTRODUCTION TO PARAGRAPHS

PSYCHOLOGY: CHARACTERISTICS OF SUCCESS

"Don't aim for success if you want it; just do what you love and believe in it, and it will come naturally."

David Frost (1939–2013)

About the Author:

David Frost was a British TV presenter and interviewer. He was best known for his interviews with famous politicians.

Work with a partner. Read the quotation about success. Then answer the questions.

1 Do you agree with David Frost? Does success come naturally?

2 What other factors do you think help people succeed?

Ⓐ Connect to Academic Writing

In this unit, you will learn the skills you need to write a paragraph. You will also learn how to organize your ideas and support them around a main idea. While some of the writing skills that you will learn may seem new to you, the skill of organizing your ideas is not new. In your everyday life you organize your ideas when you make plans for the weekend or make a shopping list.

Ⓑ Reflect on the Topic

In this section, you will look at a writing prompt and reflect on it. Throughout the unit, you will develop ideas about this prompt. You will use these ideas to practice skills that are necessary to write your paragraph.

The writing prompt below was used for the Student Model paragraph on page 50. The student reflected on his topic and used a cluster diagram to brainstorm ideas about the characteristics of a successful student.

WRITING PROMPT: Success can mean different things to different people. What three things would you like to be successful at? Use specific details and reasons to support your choice.

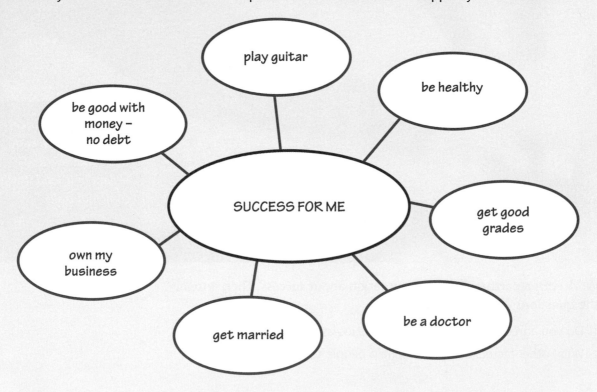

 1.1 Notice

Tell your partner about two more characteristics you could add to the cluster diagram. Share them with the class.

1.2 Apply It to Your Writing

Read the prompt and follow the directions below.

WRITING PROMPT: Success can be shown in different ways. Describe the characteristics of a successful person you know.

1 Think about all the characteristics of a successful person (for example: personality traits, talents or abilities, knowledge or intelligence).

2 Write the characteristics in the other circles.

3 Compare cluster diagrams with a partner.

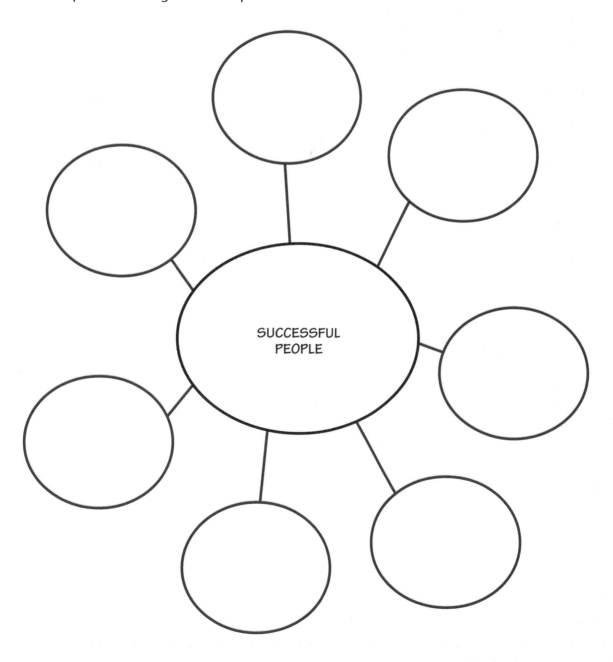

SUCCESSFUL
PEOPLE

In this section, you will learn academic language that you can use in your paragraph. You will also notice how a professional writer uses this language.

Ⓐ Academic Vocabulary

The words below appear throughout the unit. They are from the Academic Word List or the General Service List. Using these words in your writing will make your ideas clearer and your writing more academic.

achievement (n)	background (n)	effort (n)	priority (n)
analyze (v)	characteristic (n)	goal (n)	successful (adj)

 2.1 Focus on Meaning

Work with a partner. Match the words in bold to their meanings. Write the letters.

A

.... 1 My greatest **achievement** was getting 100% on my test. It's the best possible grade.

a something you accomplished

.... 2 Students who do well are often confident. Confidence is one **characteristic** that successful students share.

b an attempt to do something

.... 3 Salina makes an **effort** to learn new skills at her part-time job after school.

c to examine carefully

.... 4 Mikhail **analyzed** the results of his research so he can write a good report.

d something that is typical of a person or thing

B

.... 1 My **goal** is to get a college degree in biology.

a a person's education, family, and experience

.... 2 Melissa comes from a good educational **background**. Her parents are both teachers, and her older brother goes to college.

b something that is more important than other things

.... 3 My first **priority** is to prepare for the test. Then, I will do other less important activities.

c achieving the results you want

.... 4 After my brother finished school, he became a **successful** doctor. He has his own medical practice.

d something you want to do successfully in the future

B Academic Phrases

Research tells us that the phrases below are commonly used in academic writing.

ACTIVITY 2.2 Focus on Use

Work with a partner. Complete the paragraph using each academic phrase from the box.

It is important to	One of the most important	Part of the problem

A Big Success

Robert Pershing Wadlow was a big success. Wadlow was the tallest person in history. He was 8'11" and was still growing at the time of his death in 1940. .... (1) things to know is that Wadlow had a medical condition that caused him to grow so tall. .... (2) was that there was no treatment for this condition when he was alive. He was known as the Gentle Giant because he was very quiet and nice to everyone. Wadlow became very successful and traveled for the shoe company that made his special shoes. .... (3) remember that Wadlow was an inspiration to many people.

C Writing in the Real World

You will read an article titled "Space Diving Team." The author of the article organizes her ideas clearly to make sure that her reader understands them.

Before you read, answer this question: Can people be successful without help?

Now read the article. Think about your answer to the question as you read.

SPACE DIVING TEAM

Felix Baumgartner sits in a capsule[1] 24 miles above the Earth – the edge of space. He jumps out. Ten minutes later he lands on the ground and punches the air in delight. His record-breaking space dive becomes famous. But, while the jump only took minutes, it took many years – and many people – to prepare.

by Judy O'Lear

1   Felix Baumgartner is a skydiver and daredevil[2] from Austria. He has a military **background** where he learned the skills for the record-breaking stunts he performs. For example, he set a world record for the highest parachute jump from a building. He was also the first person to skydive across the English Channel. To achieve this **goal**, he used wings made out of special material. One of his most famous tricks was in October of 2012. Baumgartner jumped out of a capsule high above the Earth and survived.

2   Felix could not have done his **successful** space jump on his own. He needed the **efforts** of a team of 300 people for five years before he jumped out of the capsule. For example, doctors **analyzed** how his body would react to falling at over 800 miles per hour. Felix needed engineers, too. With the information from the doctors, engineers built a special space suit for Felix to wear. The engineers also built the capsule and helium[3] balloon that Felix used.

3   Felix had the **characteristics** to be successful, but he also needed people to help him on the day of the jump. Safety was a **priority**, so scientists monitored the weather conditions every minute. A team of technicians monitored Felix from the ground. They gave him step-by-step directions to help him make the perfect jump. Without this help, he would not have survived. In addition, media professionals recorded the jump and posted updates online.

4   Success requires the help and support of other people. Felix's **achievement** was amazing – but it also belongs to the team who helped him.

[1] **capsule**: the part of a spacecraft that people live in
[2] **daredevil**: someone who enjoys doing dangerous things
[3] **helium**: a gas that is lighter than air and that will not burn

 2.3 Check Your Understanding

Answer the questions.

1 The author gives examples of Felix's record-breaking stunts. Which stunt do you think is most interesting?

2 The article explains that many people helped Felix prepare for his jump. Put a check (✓) next to the people who helped him prepare.

☐ a astronauts   ☐ d family

☐ b doctors   ☐ e scientists

☐ c engineers   ☐ f technicians

3 How many people help you to be successful? Who are they?

 2.4 Notice the Features of Paragraph Writing

Answer the questions.

1 Read the second paragraph. Which sentence tells you the main idea of the paragraph?

2 Read the first paragraph again. How many examples of record-breaking stunts does the writer give?

3 What is the writer's conclusion at the end of the article?

In Section 1, you saw how the writer of the Student Model reflected on his topic. In this section, you will analyze the final draft of his paragraph. You will learn how to develop ideas for your own paragraph.

A Student Model

Read the prompt and answer the questions.

WRITING PROMPT: What three things would you like to be successful at? Use specific details and reasons to support your choice.

1 Read the title of the Student Model. What three areas of his life will the writer discuss?

2 What do you think the writer will say about these three areas?

Read the paragraph twice. The first time, think about your answers to the questions above. The second time, answer the questions in the Analyze Writing Skills boxes. This will help you notice key features of a paragraph.

Success at Work, at Play, and with Money

There are three parts of my life I want to be **successful** at. First, I want to be successful at my career. I want to be a doctor and work in my community. It is very hard to find good doctors that really help people, so I want to make sure I am there for my patients. For example, I will spend time with my patients and help them understand their illness. Second, I want to be really good at playing the guitar. I do not want to be in a band or to play professionally, but I would like to play for fun. For example, I would like to play guitar for my family and friends when we are all together. Third, my biggest **priority** is that I want to be successful with my money and have no debt. Part of the reason this is important to me is because I grew up very poor. For instance, I never had new clothes and sometimes I had to borrow money to buy my lunch or school books, which made me unhappy. In conclusion, the three things I want to be successful at are my career, my hobby, and my finances.

1 Analyze Writing Skills

Underline the sentence that tells what this paragraph will be about.

2 Analyze Writing Skills

Circle the word that introduces the first idea.

3 Analyze Writing Skills

Underline the second idea that the writer gives. Double underline the explanation and circle the examples.

4 Analyze Writing Skills

Circle the word the writer uses to introduce the third idea.

5 Analyze Writing Skills

Circle the phrase the writer uses to introduce the last sentence.

Answer the questions.

1 What are the three things the writer lists?

2 Do you agree that the things the writer chose are important?

3 What is one common goal that you would add to the paragraph?

 3.2 Outline the Writer's Ideas

Complete the outline for "Success at Work, at Play, and with Money." Use the words and phrases in the box.

finances	play for friends and family
never had new clothes, had to borrow money	spend time with patients
not in band, play for fun	

PARAGRAPH OUTLINE

First Sentence	There are three things I would like to be successful at in my life.
1st Idea	A. Career
Explanation	1. Be a doctor who really helps people
Example	2.
2nd Idea	B. Playing guitar
Explanation	1.
Example	2.
3rd Idea	C.
Explanation	1. Grew up poor
Example	2.
Last Sentence	In conclusion, the three things I want to be successful at are my career, my hobby, and my finances.

B The Paragraph

A paragraph is a group of sentences about one idea. This idea is called the main idea. All of the sentences are connected to the main idea. A good paragraph has three parts:

- a **topic sentence**
- **supporting sentences and details**
- a **concluding sentence**

An easy way to picture the order of ideas in a paragraph is to think of a sandwich. A sandwich has two slices of bread (the topic and concluding sentences). The main part of the sandwich is the filling (the supporting sentences and details).

Topic sentence: *There are three things I would like to be successful at in my life.*

Supporting sentence 1: *First...*
Detail: *I want...*   **Detail:** *It is very hard...*   **Detail:** *For example...*

Supporting sentence 2: *Second...*
Detail: *I do not want...*   **Detail:** *For example...*

Supporting sentence 3: *Third, the most important thing...*
Detail: *Part of the reason...*   **Detail:** *For instance...*

Concluding sentence: *In conclusion, the three things I want to be successful at are my career, my hobby, and my finances.*

 3.3 Notice

Look at the sandwich. Read and circle the correct answers.

1 The supporting sentences **are related / are not related** to the topic.

2 The writer **always / sometimes** added an example for each reason.

3 The ideas in the topic sentence and the concluding sentence are **similar / different**.

3.4 Identify the Sentences

Write *TS* for the topic sentence, *SS* for supporting sentences, or *CS* for the concluding sentence. Then, on a separate sheet of paper, write the sentences in the correct order to create a short paragraph.

.... 1 First, successful students get good grades. They study hard and earn high marks in their classes. They usually win awards.

.... 2 In conclusion, there are several characteristics that successful students share.

.... 3 Successful students share three characteristics.

.... 4 Also, successful students do extracurricular activities. For example, they play on one of the school's sports teams, are a member of a club, or play an instrument in the school band.

.... 5 Finally, successful students have excellent attendance. They rarely miss classes, even when they feel tired.

THE TOPIC SENTENCE

The topic sentence introduces the **main idea**. A topic sentence relates to the question in the writing prompt. There are two parts of a topic sentence:

- the topic
- the controlling idea

The **topic** is the general idea. It tells the reader what the paragraph is about. The **controlling idea** is more specific. It tells the reader what kind of information about the topic is in the paragraph. Read the topic sentences below and notice the two parts.

TOPIC (GENERAL)   CONTROLLING IDEA (SPECIFIC)
Robert Pershing Wadlow <u>was a big success</u>.

CONTROLLING IDEA (SPECIFIC)   TOPIC (GENERAL)
<u>There are important benefits</u> to being a part of a team.

 3.5 Identify Topics and Controlling Ideas

Circle the topic in each sentence. Underline the controlling idea.

1 My greatest personal success was teaching my brother how to ride a bike.

2 There are benefits to failing before you succeed.

3 One of the most successful people I know is my father.

4 Bill Gates is one of the most successful businesspeople in history.

5 There are three strategies to successfully learn a second language.

6 Being successful requires a team of people.

7 I believe you can learn three lessons from failing before you succeed.

8 The most popular videos on YouTube share several characteristics.

MORE ABOUT CONTROLLING IDEAS

Many controlling ideas for each topic are possible. For example, the topic of the Student Model on page 50 is personal success. The controlling idea is about the different ways to achieve personal success.

Think about the topic of success. You could write about many ideas. For example:

Success changes people for the better

Success requires people to follow three steps

Money is not the only measure of success

Success takes a lot of effort

Below is the topic "Successful Businesspeople" and five possible controlling ideas.

TOPIC (GENERAL)	CONTROLLING IDEA (SPECIFIC)
Successful businesspeople	*share three characteristics*
	have a wide variety of relationships
	are focused on more than just money
	make positive contributions to the world

The writing prompt will determine the choices that you have for your controlling ideas. You will learn more about topic sentences in Section 4 of this unit.

 3.6 Identifying Controlling Ideas

Read each writing prompt and complete the topic sentence with a controlling idea. You can use the ideas from the "success" topic to help.

1 What characteristics do successful parents have?

Successful parents ....

....

2 Does success change people? In what way?

Success changes people ....

....

3 How do you achieve your goals?

Achieving your goals requires ....

....

4 Can failure ever be a good thing? Why or why not?

Failure ....

....

5 Some people say success comes naturally. Do you agree or disagree? Support your answer.

Many people think that success ....

....

ACTIVITY **3.7** Apply It to Your Writing

YOUR TURN

Think about your writing prompt on page 45. Write a topic sentence. Then trade sentences with a partner. Tell your partner what information you think he or she will include in the paragraph.

....

....

....

....

SUPPORTING SENTENCES AND DETAILS

The **supporting sentences** are in the middle of the paragraph. They help readers understand more about the topic sentence. They make the topic sentence clear and convincing to readers. All the supporting sentences should be related to the topic sentence.

Writers sometimes organize their supporting sentences by **ranking** them. Ranking means putting ideas in a particular order of importance. Writers usually use certain words and phrases to rank sentences.

First, …

The first [characteristic] is …

Second, …

The next [factor] is …

Third, …

The most important [reason] is …

Look at the supporting sentences for the topic sentence below. All of these supporting sentences help explain the characteristics of successful students.

Successful students share three characteristics: they get good grades, do extracurricular activities, and have excellent attendance.

First, successful students get good grades.

Also, successful students do extracurricular activities.

Finally, successful students have perfect attendance.

As you learned in Unit 1, writers also include extra information to illustrate their ideas.

They include details, such as examples, explanations, and reasons. Writers sometimes include one or two details after each supporting sentence. Look at the <u>underlined</u> details after each supporting sentence in this draft paragraph:

Characteristics of Successful Students

Successful students share three characteristics. First, successful students get good grades. <u>They study hard and earn high marks in their classes. They usually win awards.</u> Also, successful students do extracurricular activities. <u>For example, they play on one of the school's sports teams, are a member of a club, or play an instrument in the school band.</u> Finally, successful students have perfect attendance. <u>They rarely miss classes, even when they feel tired from work.</u> In conclusion, there are several ways successful students are the same.

ACTIVITY **3.8** Notice

Look at the Student Model on page 50. Check (✓) the ideas the writer included.

☐ 1 career success   ☐ 4 help patients

☐ 2 play music for friends   ☐ 5 play guitar

☐ 3 have no debt   ☐ 6 borrow clothes

ACTIVITY **3.9** Recognize Supporting Sentences

Work with a partner. Underline the supporting sentences.

Success Is More Than Luck

It takes more than luck to become successful. First, to be successful you need a clear goal. Successful people know exactly what they want to achieve and how they are going to do it. For example, my brother knew he wanted to get a degree in pharmacology and work as a pharmacist. He planned everything very carefully, such as the courses he would take and the tests he needed to pass. Now he is a pharmacist at the largest pharmacy in the city. Second, being successful requires focus. Successful people do not get distracted by things that are not related to their goals. For example, my brother spent a lot of time studying and did not go out with his friends very often. Third, being successful requires confidence. People who do not believe in themselves cannot become successful. Successful people think positively and know that they can achieve their goals. My brother always had a good attitude and knew he could become a pharmacist if he worked hard. He did not believe anyone who said it would be too hard. In conclusion, success is not just about luck; it requires specific goals, focus, and confidence.

ACTIVITY **3.10** Write Supporting Sentences

Read the topic sentence and concluding sentence. Add supporting sentences using the characteristics mentioned in the concluding sentence.

What Makes a Movie Successful?

In order for a movie to be successful, it must have three characteristics. First, ...

....

This means there should be lots of exciting and entertaining scenes. Next, ...

....

The best movies tell an interesting or unusual story. The most important thing is ....

....

Most people want to see a movie that has famous actors in it. In summary, a movie should have a lot of action, a good plot, and movie stars.

3.11 Write Details

Add a detail (a–c) to each of the supporting sentences in the paragraph below.
Write the letters.

a As a result, I now have almost a thousand dollars saved that can help me pay for college.

b For example, my mother stayed home with me when my team lost the championship baseball game.

c To illustrate, my mother fixed me chicken soup and took my temperature whenever I did not feel well.

My mother was successful for several reasons. First, she was always there for me when I was

sad. .... Second, she took good care of me when I was sick. .... The most important
(1)   (2)

thing my mother did was she saved money in a bank account for me. .... In conclusion,
(3)

my mother was a success to me because she was always there for me, took care of me,

and saved money for me.

 3.12 Write Supporting Sentences and Details

Work with a partner. On a separate piece of paper, write your own paragraph titled
"What Makes a Movie Successful?" Include three supporting sentences and a detail
for each.

 3.13 Apply It to Your Writing

YOUR
TURN

Work with a partner. Go to the topic sentence you wrote for Activity 3.7 on page 55.
Write a supporting sentence and some details for one idea in your topic sentence.

THE CONCLUDING SENTENCE

The **concluding sentence** is the last sentence in the paragraph. The concluding sentence often restates, or repeats, the topic sentence using different words. Writers do not include any new ideas in the concluding sentence. For example:

In conclusion, there are several characteristics that successful students share.

Sometimes the concluding sentence summarizes the main points from the supporting sentences:

In conclusion, success is not just about luck; it requires specific goals, focus, and confidence.

Writers often use certain phrases to introduce the concluding sentence:

In conclusion, …, In summary, …, In brief, …, In short, …

 3.14 Identify Concluding Sentences

Work with a partner. Read these topic sentences. Circle the concluding sentence that best restates the topic sentence.

1 Topic Sentence: People do certain things to make sure a marriage is successful.

   a In conclusion, marriages are not very successful.

   b In conclusion, listening to your spouse is one thing people can do for a successful marriage.

   c In conclusion, marriages can become more successful by doing certain things.

2 Topic Sentence: There are obstacles beyond our control that can prevent success.

   a In conclusion, sometimes we can control our own success.

   b In summary, you will face a lot of obstacles.

   c In brief, there are a lot of obstacles that prevent success.

3 Topic Sentence: I learned three things from failure.

   a In conclusion, failure is usually negative.

   b In short, failure taught me several things.

   c In summary, many people have failed.

3.15 Write a Concluding Sentence

Write a concluding sentence for the paragraph below.

Planning a Successful Vacation

Having a great vacation is more likely if you plan three things in advance. First, you should plan your accommodations. For example, if you are staying in a hotel, you should make a reservation. If you are staying at someone's house, you need to confirm the dates. One of the most important things you should plan in advance is your transportation. For instance, you need to make flight reservations if you are traveling to a place that is too far to drive to. If you are driving, decide if you need to rent a car. Third, buy tickets for theme parks, museums, and other tourist attractions before you leave. Part of the reason you want to do this is so that the location will not be sold out when you arrive. Sometimes you get a better price, too. ....

....

....

 3.16 Apply It to Your Writing

Think about the topic sentence that you wrote in Activity 3.7 on page 57.
Write two different concluding sentences you could use in your final paragraph.

....

....

....

....

....

Ⓐ Writing Skill 1: Writing Good Topic Sentences

In Section 3, you learned that a topic sentence includes a topic and a controlling idea. A good topic sentence has three main characteristics:

- It controls the whole paragraph.
- It is not too general.
- It is not too specific.

Think about the topic "the English language." Which of the topic sentences below includes the best controlling idea?

English is hard.

English borrows words from French.

English is the best language to learn for several reasons.

The first topic sentence is too general. It does not have any specific ideas and does not tell the reader why English is hard. The second topic sentence is too specific. This could be one idea of the paragraph, but it does not mention other ideas in the paragraph (i.e., other characteristics of English). The third topic sentence is the best topic sentence. The reader will expect several reasons why English is the best language to learn.

 4.1 Recognize Good Topic Sentences

Read each topic and write an *S* next to the topic sentence that is too specific, a *G* next to the topic sentence that is too general, and a *B* next to the topic sentence that is the best choice.

1 A successful life

.... Money is a good measure of a successful life.

.... A successful life is measured by professional and personal achievements.

.... It is easy to have a successful life.

2 The United States

.... The United States has a large population.

.... The United States is a country in North America.

.... The United States is home to people from many nations.

3 Debating

.... Debating is a good skill to have for many reasons.

.... You need good communication skills to debate.

.... Debating is fun.

4 Tea

.... Tea tastes good.

.... Tea has several health benefits.

.... Tea contains too much caffeine.

5 Museums

.... Museums have paintings.

.... Museums contain several different types of art.

.... Museums are interesting.

ACTIVITY **4.2** **Write Topic Sentences**

Use your own ideas to write a topic sentence for each topic.

1 Failure

2 Successful businesses

3 A good doctor

4 Good public transportation

5 Soccer

4.3 Write Topic Sentences

Read the paragraph about people who failed before finding success. Write a good topic sentence for it.

Failure Before Success

....

....

One person who failed before becoming successful is Steven Spielberg. The University of Southern California rejected him three times. He then became a famous movie director. Another person who failed before becoming famous is the actor Harrison Ford. People told him he did not have the qualities he needed to be a movie star. He then went on to star in films such as *Star Wars* and *Indiana Jones*. He has been nominated for several acting awards. A third example is the inventor of the lightbulb, Thomas Edison. Teachers told him he would not succeed, and he was fired from several jobs. He even had many unsuccessful tries at inventing the lightbulb. We still use the lightbulb and many of his other inventions today. In conclusion, we sometimes fail before we succeed.

B Writing Skill 2: Titles

A good title tells the readers what they will find in the paragraph. It also makes readers curious about the topic so they want to read the paragraph.

CHOOSING TITLES	
1 Titles are short phrases. They are not sentences.	~~Successful Engineers Have Several Characteristics~~ *Characteristics of Successful Engineers*
2 Good titles tell the reader the main idea. They are not too general or too specific.	GOOD TITLE: *Characteristics of Successful Engineers* TOO SPECIFIC: *Successful Engineers Are Smart, Team Players, and Good Networkers* TOO GENERAL: *Successful Engineers*

FORMATTING TITLES	
1 Center titles over the paragraph.	*Measuring Success* *There are several ways to measure success …*
2 Capitalize nouns, verbs, adjectives, and adverbs. Do not capitalize prepositions, conjunctions (*and* and *but*), or articles (*a/an, the*) unless they are the first word in the title.	NOUN PREP ADJ NOUN *Characteristics of Successful Engineers* VERB NOUN *Measuring Success*
3 Do not put a period at the end of a title.	*A Successful Marriage.*

ACTIVITY 4.4 Select Titles

Imagine you wrote a paragraph about a dinner you had at an award-winning new restaurant and you did not like the food, service, or atmosphere. Choose which titles are unacceptable (*U*) and which are acceptable (*A*).

.... 1 A New Restaurant

.... 2 Eating

.... 3 My Experience at a New Restaurant

.... 4 I Hated the New Restaurant

.... 5 The Food, Service, and Atmosphere at a New Restaurant

.... 6 A Bad Experience at a New Restaurant

Read the writing prompt and topic sentence and write a possible title. Share your title with a partner. Choose one to share with the class.

1 **WRITING PROMPT**: In some countries, students work part-time while they are in school. Do you think this is a good idea? Support your opinion by using specific reasons and details.

Topic Sentence: I believe that working part-time while going to school is a good idea because it promotes hard work, improves time management, and encourages responsibility.

Title: ....

2 **WRITING PROMPT**: Some people believe that success in life comes from taking chances. Others believe that success results from careful planning. What does success come from?

Topic Sentence: I think that success in life is the result of careful planning.

Title: ....

3 **WRITING PROMPT**: Do you agree or disagree with the following statement: Friends are a more important influence than parents on a child's success in school. Use specific reasons and examples to support your answer.

Topic Sentence: In my opinion, parents are the greatest influence on a child's success in school.

Title: ....

C Grammar for Writing: Common Verb + Preposition Combinations

Some verbs are usually followed by certain prepositions.

COMMON VERB + PREPOSITION COMBINATIONS	
get ahead + of	*Successful companies **get ahead of** their competition.*
commit + to	*Successful police officers **commit to** upholding the law.*
focus + on	*Successful teachers **focus on** their students.*
care + about	*Successful doctors **care about** their patients.*
learn + from	*Successful managers **learn from** their mistakes.*
look + for	*Successful coaches **look for** ways to win games.*
work + for	*Successful stores **work for** their customers' loyalty.*
take care + of	*Successful mothers **take care of** their children.*

ACTIVITY **4.6** Write Verb + Preposition Combinations

A Read each sentence. Choose the correct verb from the box.

commit to	focuses on	look for	work for

1 Many people .... big companies because they often get better benefits.

2 You can .... more information about famous inventors online.

3 If you want to get into a good college, ... studying hard.

4 The new documentary about Felix Baumgartner .... his recent stunts.

B Read each sentence. Choose the correct verb from the box.

cares about	get ahead of	learn from	takes care of

1 A babysitter .... children until their parents return.

2 Some students like to .... e-books because e-books are easier to carry.

3 Business need to take risks if they want to .... the competition.

4 He .... getting good grades because he wants to go to a good university.

Avoiding Common Mistakes

Research tells us that these are the most common mistakes that students make when using verb + preposition combinations in academic writing.

> **1 Remember to use a preposition with certain verbs.**
>
>   *for*
> People need to look˰ways to improve their skills.
>
> **2 Do not confuse *get ahead* with *go ahead*.**
>
>   *get*
> You need to work hard if you want to ~~go~~ ahead in your career.
>
> **3 Remember to use *of* and not *about* with *take care of*.**
>
>   *of*
> People need to take care ~~about~~ their health in order to do well in school and work.

 4.7 Editing Task

Find and correct four more mistakes in the paragraph below.

Famous Failures

    Success does not mean winning all the time. There are some very successful people who failed before becoming famous and successful. They stayed committed ~~with~~ *to* their goals and kept trying. The first example is Steve Jobs. When Jobs was younger, he was fired from Apple, the company he started. However, he stayed focused to business. He started another company, bought a movie company, and invented some of the electronics millions of people use today. The second example is Walt Disney. Walt Disney worked to a newspaper. He was fired because the manager did not think he had enough imagination or original ideas. Despite this failure, Walt Disney focused about his goal and proved that he had a lot of imagination by starting Disneyland, Disney World, and EPCOT. People think he was one of the most creative people who ever lived. The third example is Oprah Winfrey. She was a news anchor for a television station. The managers did not like her work. They said she cried too much and did not look good on television. She did not let the failure stop her in achieving success. Later, her talk show was one of the most watched shows on television. In conclusion, even some of the most successful people have failed on their road to success.

ⓓ Avoiding Plagiarism

When you write a college assignment, you should use your own ideas and words.

I am worried. I often cannot write my thoughts in English, and I do not want to make a mistake when I write. Sometimes I like to use other people's words. Their words express my ideas. They say them more clearly than I do, but my teacher says I am plagiarizing. I don't understand.

– Roberto

Dear Roberto,

Do you play soccer? Maybe you do. Do you play like the Argentinian superstar Lionel Messi? You probably don't. However, you still play the game and work towards improving your skills. It is the same in writing. You might find a really good author. You like the author's ideas, but you can't just use his or her words. If you just use someone else's words or ideas, it is wrong. You need to think for yourself and say things in your own words. Your instructors enjoy reading your ideas and helping you become the best writer you can be.

Yours truly,

Professor Wright

STRATEGIES TO AVOID PLAGIARISM

Here are some common thoughts that students have about writing. Think about your last writing assignment. Were any of these true for you?

☐ I can't express my ideas well in English.

☐ I need to get a good grade.

☐ I don't have enough time to do this writing assignment.

Sometimes students plagiarize for the reasons above. On the next page are some strategies to help you avoid plagiarizing for those reasons.

STRATEGIES FOR AVOIDING PLAGIARISM

STRATEGY	RESULT
Read about your topic and discuss the ideas with someone in English.	You will develop confidence in expressing your ideas.
Go to your school's Writing Center, or ask someone to read a draft of your ideas.	This can help you improve your grade because you will improve your writing.
Make a schedule. Write a little bit every day.	You will have time to complete the assignment and decrease the pressure to meet deadlines.

 4.8 Practice

Work with a partner.

1 Choose two strategies from the chart above that you think will help you. Why did you choose them? How can they help you on your next assignment?

2 With your partner, think of another reason a student might plagiarize. What strategy could avoid this? Share your ideas with the class.

In this section, you will follow the writing process to complete the final draft of your paragraph.

STEP 1: BRAINSTORM

In this unit, you will continue your brainstorm using a T-chart. T-charts are boxes with two sides that you fill in with your ideas. You can label the boxes so that each box is about a different part of your topic. This will help you to brainstorm more and begin to organize your ideas.

Work with a partner. Follow the steps below to brainstorm more ideas for your topic.

1 First, read the student's brainstorm. He wrote many ideas from the cluster diagram he used to reflect on his topic in Section 1, on page 44. Then, he created the T-chart below. Compare the information in his paragraph on page 50 to the T-chart below. The writer chose not to include some of the ideas. Why do you think he made that choice?

SUCCESS	
PROFESSIONAL	**PERSONAL**
Be a doctor Own my business	Play guitar Get married Be healthy No debt

2 Now read your writing prompt again. Then review the ideas that you brainstormed in Section 1, page 45. Write the best ones in the T-chart below. Add ideas from the Your Turns that you completed in the unit. Finally, brainstorm more ideas. You will probably not use every idea, but it is good to write as many ideas as possible.

SUCCESSFUL PEOPLE	
CHARACTERISTICS	**DETAILS**

STEP 2: MAKE AN OUTLINE

Complete the outline below with ideas for your paragraph from Step 1.

PARAGRAPH OUTLINE

Topic Sentence	
1st Idea	A.
Detail	1.
Detail	2.
2nd Idea	B.
Detail	1.
Detail	2.
3rd Idea	C.
Detail	1.
Detail	2.
Concluding Sentence	

STEP 3: WRITE YOUR FIRST DRAFT

Now it is time to write your first draft. Here are some suggestions on how to get started.

1 Use your outline and the sentences you wrote in the Your Turns and in Step 2 above.

2 Focus on making your ideas as clear as possible.

3 Add a title.

After you finish, read your paragraph and check for basic errors.

1 Check that all sentences have subjects and verbs.

2 Go through and look at every comma. Is it correct? Should it be a period?

3 Check that you have used a comma after adverb clauses when they start a sentence.

4 Make sure your topic sentence and supporting sentences are clear.

STEP 4: WRITE YOUR FINAL DRAFT

1 After you receive feedback on your first draft, review it carefully. Fix any errors.

2 Make a note of errors that were most frequent (misspellings, using commas instead of periods, missing verbs). Try to avoid them as you write.

3 Review the Academic Vocabulary and Phrases from this unit. Are there any that you can add to your paragraph?

4 Turn to page 238 and use the Self-Editing Review to check your work one more time.

5 Write your final draft and hand it in.

3 NARRATIVE PARAGRAPHS

HEALTH: HEALTH BEHAVIORS

> *"Health is not valued until sickness comes."*
>
> Thomas Fuller
> (1608–1661)

About the Author:

Thomas Fuller was an English historian.

Work with a partner. Read the quotation about health. Then answer the questions.

1 Do you think about your health only when you get sick?

2 What do you do to keep healthy?

Ⓐ Connect to Academic Writing

In this unit, you will learn skills to organize your ideas and support them in a narrative paragraph. While some of these skills may seem new to you, in your everyday life you often tell stories. For example, you might describe how you bought a new car or tell about how you got your first job. The narrative can inform or entertain the reader. It can also support your opinion and convince the reader to agree with you.

Ⓑ Reflect on the Topic

In this section, you will look at a writing prompt and reflect on it. Throughout the unit, you will develop ideas about this prompt. You will use these ideas to practice skills that are necessary to write your paragraph.

The writing prompt below was used for the Student Model paragraph on page 80. The student reflected on the topic and used a freewrite to brainstorm someone who inspired him.

STUDENT MODEL

WRITING PROMPT: Tell the story of someone who changed to a healthier lifestyle. You can tell your own story or the story of someone you know.

My father had heart attack. I was 19. This saved my life. (It saved his life, too.) I was overweight when was growing up. I was unhealthy. My father he was unhealthy, too. He was overweight. He didn't exercise. Then—wow!—the heart attack. He was in the hospital. Then he came home, and we decided to improve our lives.. 1) We started walking together four days a week—then running 2) We started eating vegetables and chicken or fish a lot. We lost over 250 pounds for the both of us..

ACTIVITY **1.1** Notice

Work with a partner. Who is this story about? What's the first thing that happened in the story? What's the last thing?

Read the prompt and follow the directions below.

WRITING PROMPT: Who is someone who inspired you because of the way that they recovered from an illness or accident? Tell their story.

1 Choose someone who has had an illness or an accident. It could be someone you know or someone from the news.

2 Think about what happened to this person before, during, and after his or her illness or accident. Use the space below to quickly write down – freewrite – this story.

3 Compare your freewrite with a partner.

In this section, you will learn academic language that you can use in your narrative paragraph. You will also notice how a professional writer uses this language.

Ⓐ Academic Vocabulary

The words below appear throughout the unit. They are from the Academic Word List or the General Service List. Using these words in your writing will make your ideas clearer and your writing more academic.

attitude (n)	energy (n)	improvement (n)	quality (n)
brain (n)	healthy (adj)	produce (v)	relax (v)

 2.1 Focus on Meaning

Work with a partner. Read the sentences. Decide the meaning of the words in bold and circle the correct definitions.

1 Elena has a lot of **energy**. She's busy all the time and does not often feel tired. **Energy** means

 a success in achieving goals.   b ability to be active.

2 During sleep, the **brain** is still active. Research suggests that people can still work on math problems even while they are sleeping. **Brain** means

 a organ inside the head.   b the hand that you write with.

3 Smoking cigarettes is bad for your health. There is **improvement** in your health when you stop smoking. **Improvement** means

 a something that gives someone problems.   b something that is better or makes something better.

4 Most students are stressed before an exam. They **relax** when the exam is over. **Relax** means

 a become calm and comfortable.   b begin to learn something.

5 A good **attitude** might help people recover from an accident. People who think positive thoughts seem to get well faster than people who focus on the pain. **Attitude** means

 a condition of the body.   b the way a person feels about something.

6 Do not look at a computer screen late at night. The screens **produce** light which makes it difficult to sleep. **Produce** means

 a turn off.   b make.

7 Marie was off work sick for two weeks, but now she's **healthy**. She will return to work tomorrow. **Healthy** means

 a having a good condition of the body.   b ready to work.

8 High **quality** food is essential for good health. However, some people eat too much low quality food such as soda, donuts, and potato chips. **Quality** means

 a how good or bad something is.   b with a lot of sugar or fat.

B Academic Collocations

Collocations are words that are frequently used together. Research tells us that the academic vocabulary in Part A is commonly used in the collocations in bold below.

ACTIVITY **2.2** Focus on Meaning

Work with a partner. Match the collocations in bold to their meanings. Write the letters.

.... 1 A person with a good **quality of life** is happy with his or her work, leisure, and health.

.... 2 If you have **high energy**, you can work or exercise hard and not feel tired.

.... 3 Someone with a **positive attitude** believes that good things are possible now and in the future.

.... 4 I never exercised. Then I read a report about the bad effects of not exercising that **changed my attitude**.

.... 5 When I started exercising there was a **significant improvement** in my life. I had more energy.

a a feeling of hopefulness about things

b an important, positive change

c a lot of ability to be very active

d a person's level of satisfaction and comfort

e to have a new way of thinking about things

C Writing in the Real World

You will read a blog titled "The Importance of Getting Sleep in College." The author of the blog uses a narrative to tell the reader why sleep is important.

Before you read, answer this question: How much sleep is necessary, and how can students get enough?

Now read the article. Think about your answer to the question as you read.

THE IMPORTANCE OF GETTING SLEEP IN COLLEGE

BY MARINA OLINSKY

1 Alex understood the importance of sleep in his first semester in college. As a child, Alex had a lot of **energy**. He ate well, got a good amount of exercise, and was **healthy** most of the time. Then he started college. He still ate well, but he got only about six hours of sleep each night. He was tired all the time. When he started getting bad grades, he knew something was wrong. That's when he realized he had to get more sleep.

2 Many college students have a similar experience. A study from Brown University found that 73% of college students don't get enough sleep. There are many reasons for this. First, they have homework to do and exams to study for. They're also making new friends and want to spend time with them. In addition, many students have to work part-time jobs to help pay for college. For these reasons, and many others, many students do not get the eight hours of sleep they typically need.

3   For many reasons, sleep is essential for a good **quality** of life. First, it is important for good physical health. For example, it allows the body to fight off sickness. It gives the heart a rest. Second, sleep is necessary for clear thinking. The **brain** is actively working during sleep. This helps people to learn and remember things when they are awake. Third, sleep can help fight off emotional problems such as depression or sadness. And of course, restful sleep makes everyone look and feel better the next day.

4   Many students think they can catch up[1] on sleep over the weekend. Unfortunately, this doesn't work. It can cause *more* sleep problems. Recent research suggests that students should follow these four steps to improve their quality of sleep. Each day, they should spend some time outside. It is also important to get daily exercise (but not just before going to sleep). They should avoid[2] caffeine in coffee or tea after lunchtime. They should avoid TV and cell phone screens at night because the light they **produce** keeps people awake. Also, it is good to go to sleep and wake up at about the same time every day.

5   If students follow these suggestions, they will notice a significant **improvement** in their sleep and their life in general.

[1] **catch up (on):** do something you did not have time to do earlier
[2] **avoid:** stay away from

 2.3 Check Your Understanding

Answer the questions.

1   What problem did Alex have that many college students have?

2   Why is sleep essential?

3   How many steps should you take if you want to get enough sleep?

 2.4 Notice the Features of Narrative Writing

Answer the questions.

1   Read the first paragraph again. Underline the words that tell you the main idea of the paragraph.

2   Check (✓) which sentence from the reading happens first in time. How do you know?

   ☐ a   Alex understood the importance of sleep in his first semester in college.

   ☐ b   As a child, Alex had a lot of energy.

3   What word is the same in the first and last sentences of the first paragraph?

In Section 1, you saw how the writer of the Student Model reflected on his topic. In this section, you will analyze the final draft of his paragraph. You will learn how to develop ideas for your own paragraph.

Ⓐ Student Model

Read the prompt and answer the questions.

WRITING PROMPT: Tell the story of someone who changed to a healthier lifestyle. You can tell your own story or the story of someone you know.

1　Read the title of the Student Model. Who is the writer going to write about?

2　What story do you think the writer will tell?

Read the paragraph twice. The first time, think about your answers to the questions above. The second time, answer the questions in the Analyze Writing Skills boxes. This will help you notice key features of a narrative paragraph.

My Father, the Life-Saver

When I was 19 years old, my father saved my life by having a heart attack. I was overweight when I was growing up, and my **quality** of life was terrible. All I did was **relax** at home, eat, and play video games. I was very unhealthy. My father was unhealthy, too. Like me, he was overweight and did not exercise. Then he had his heart attack. It was a big shock for both of us. After he came home from the hospital, we decided to make significant **improvements** to our quality of life. We got **healthy** together. First, we started eating vegetables and chicken or fish for every meal. At this time, we also started walking together four days a week. After a few months, we were running. Together, we lost over 250 pounds! One of the most important things we did was change our **attitude**. Now we believe in the value of a healthy lifestyle. I say my dad saved my life, but he says I saved his, too.

1 Analyze Writing Skills

Circle the event that changed the person's life.

2 Analyze Writing Skills

Underline the sentences about life before the father's heart attack.

3 Analyze Writing Skills

Double underline the first event after the hospital.

4 Analyze Writing Skills

What information is the same as in the topic sentence? Circle it.

3.1 Check Your Understanding

Answer the questions.

1 What was similar about the writer's life and his father's life when the writer was growing up?

2 What caused them both to make a big change? What changes did they make?

3 Have you ever experienced something bad that caused you to make a good change? If so, what happened?

 3.2 Outline the Writer's Ideas

Complete the outline for "My Father, the Life-Saver." Use the words and phrases in the box.

father's heart attack	overweight and did not exercise	started walking, then running
got healthy again	quality of life terrible	vegetables, chicken, and fish

PARAGRAPH OUTLINE

Topic Sentence	When I was 19 years old, my father saved my life by having a heart attack.
1st Event	A.
Detail	1. Just relaxed, ate, and played video games
Detail	2. Father was unhealthy, too
Detail	3.
2nd Event	B.
Detail	1. Big shock
Detail	2. Got healthy together
Final Event	C.
Detail	1. Started eating well
Detail	2.

Detail	3. ....
Detail	4. Lost over 250 pounds ....
Concluding Sentences	One of the most important things we did was change our attitude. I say my dad saved my life, but he says I saved his, too.

B Narrative Paragraphs

A narrative is a story or a description of a series of events. Writers use the narrative for different purposes: to entertain, inform, or persuade the reader. It has a beginning, middle, and end. It is usually in order of time, or **chronological order**.

 3.3 Put Events in Order

Look at the paragraph below. Then put the events (1–8) in the correct place on the timeline on page 83.

She Can Dance Again

It took almost a year, but my friend Ana was able to recover from a horrible car accident. From the age of five, Ana loved dancing. She took dance lessons through school and majored in dance in college. She was full of energy and had a positive attitude about everything. Then one day on her way to the college, she had a car crash. Ana woke up in the hospital the next day and learned she had lost her left foot. She turned her face to the wall and did not speak with any of us for days. She did not eat or read or watch TV. After several weeks, her health improved, and she moved back home, but she was terribly unhappy. Then her dance teacher came to visit her. He told her about a dance competition the next year. He wanted her to enter it. This seemed impossible to her at first, but it gave her a goal – something to focus on. She got a prosthetic foot and began physical therapy exercises six days a week. After a few weeks, there was a significant improvement in her attitude. When she took her first step on her new, prosthetic foot, her smile was like sunshine. She knew she could dance again.

1	got new prosthetic foot	5	took dance lessons
2	danced again	6	was terribly unhappy
3	had a car crash	7	had physical therapy
4	lost left foot	8	learned about a dance competition

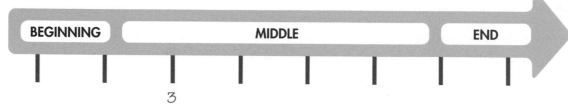

BEGINNING   MIDDLE   END

3

THE BEGINNING: TOPIC SENTENCES

In a narrative paragraph, the **topic sentence** sets up the story. It immediately answers the prompt. It gets to the important information right away. For this reason, it is not usually in the same chronological order as the rest of the story.

In the **second sentence**, the writer usually begins the story in chronological order.

 3.4 Notice

Look at the timeline in Activity 3.3. Circle the correct answers.

1 We first learn about the car accident **at the beginning / in the middle** of the paragraph.

2 The actual beginning of the story (in the order of time) is in the **first / second** sentence.

3 The car accident *happens* in the **second / fifth** sentence of the story.

3.5 Identify Topic Sentences

Read the writing prompts and sentences below. Choose the best topic sentence for each prompt. Then underline the sentence that happened first in time. Share your answers with a partner.

1 **WRITING PROMPT:** What is an experience that influenced your health habits or the health habits of someone you know? Tell this story.

   a Until last year, Lili used to have just a donut and coffee for breakfast.

   b Today, Lili has a big, healthy breakfast every morning because of one week she spent on her uncle's farm.

2 **WRITING PROMPT:** There are many popular diet trends these days. In your opinion, is there one that helps people to achieve success? If so, which one? If not, why? Tell the story of how you (or someone you know) reached this conclusion.

   a Sara recently learned that the best diet is no diet at all.

   b In high school, she wanted to be thin, so she went from one crazy diet to the next.

3 **WRITING PROMPT:** Do you believe it is important to follow directions? Give an example of a time when you did (or did not) follow directions. What happened?

   a Sometimes, not following simple directions can be dangerous.

   b One day last summer, my friend and I went for a short two-mile hike.

 3.6 Apply It to Your Writing

Think about your writing prompt in Section 1 on page 75. How does your story start? Write some possible topic sentences you could use.

THE MIDDLE

The sentences in the middle of a narrative paragraph tell the story. They explain the series of events or problem that the topic sentence introduces. The middle of the paragraph tells the story of *what happened*, in **chronological order**, or order of time. The writer of the paragraph thinks, "What happened first? And next? And after that?"

As you tell a story, you can use words and phrases to indicate the chronological order of events. Some of these words and phrases are:

First,	*Later,*	*After a while,*
At that time,	*Then*	*Next,*
One day,	*After that,*	*The next day / week / month,*

 3.7 Notice

In the paragraph below, underline the words and phrases that indicate the order of events.

The Hike That Went Wrong

Sometimes, not following simple directions can be dangerous. One day, my friend Sam and I went for a hike. At that time, we were not in good shape. The hike was short, so we thought it was no problem. That was a mistake. We made other mistakes. First, we did not notice the sign at the beginning of the hike. It had directions and a map of the trail. After a while, we started to get tired. Then we came to a place where the trail divided. We went right. Later, we learned that "right" was for the ten-mile hike. "Left" was for the short hike. We walked for a long, long time. Finally, we reached the end. The next day, we did not want to move. On that hike, we learned the importance of following directions.

3.8 Use Language of Chronological Order

Complete the paragraph with the words and phrases below to indicate the order of events. More than one answer is possible.

After a while,	First,	The next day,
~~At that time,~~	One day,	Then,

The Impossible Essay

My friend Danny learned a lesson about balance[1] near the end of his first year at the university. When he started the year, his goal was to finish in four years. ___At that time,___ (1) he enrolled in five classes. Also, he had to work twenty hours a week at a supermarket to pay the tuition.[2] It was not easy, but he had a lot of energy. To make time for classes, work, and homework, he gave up[3] several things. _____ (2) he stopped running, which he usually did five mornings a week. _____ (3) he stopped meeting his friends for pizza and a movie on Friday nights. Also, he got only five hours of sleep at night. _____ (4) he started to have health problems. He had headaches and stomach problems. He was always nervous. He could not relax. All the time, he thought, "I need to work harder," but he was very tired all the time, too. _____ (5) near the end of his second semester, something happened. He was at his desk. He was trying to write a difficult essay for class. He could not think of ideas. His brain did not seem to work. Suddenly, he thought, "I can't do this. It's impossible." He got his jacket and went for a long walk. He stopped at my house, and we had a good visit. That night, Danny slept eight hours. _____ (6) he woke up and felt much better. He says he felt free. He went to his computer and finished the "impossible" essay. That morning, he saw how important it is to balance work with other things, like exercise, friends, and sleep.

[1] **balance:** having the right amounts of different things
[2] **tuition:** money for classes, especially college or university
[3] **give up:** stop doing or having something

MORE ABOUT THE MIDDLE OF THE PARAGRAPH

The events in the middle of the paragraph include **details**. Details are specific information that helps the reader understand each event. These details also make the paragraph more interesting. Some possible details are reasons, explanations, and examples. Other details are adjectives, words that describe nouns and help the reader "see" and "feel" the picture.

Use the following questions to help you think about details for your narrative paragraphs:

1 Who was there?

2 How did the person / people feel?

3 Why did it happen?

4 How can I describe the event so that the reader can see and feel it?

5 What examples can I add?

6 Can I be specific with amounts?

 3.9 Find Details

Work with a partner. Underline the details in the paragraph that make it more interesting than the similar paragraph in Activity 3.7 on page 85. Share your ideas with a partner.

The Hike That Went Wrong

Sometimes, not following simple directions can be dangerous. One day last summer, my friend Sam and I went for a short hike. At that time, we were not very fit because we did not exercise. The hike was only two miles, so we thought it was no problem. That was a mistake. We made other mistakes. First, we did not notice the sign at the beginning of the hike. It had directions and a map of the trail. After we walked for an hour, we started to get tired. Then we came to a place where the trail divided. We went right. Later, we learned that "right" was for the ten-mile hike. "Left" was for the two-mile hike. We walked for a long, long time. We were very hot and tired. We thought we were going to die. Finally, we reached the end. All our muscles hurt. The next day, we did not want to move. On that hike, we learned the importance of following directions.

 3.10 Apply It to Your Writing

Think about your writing prompt in Section 1 on page 75. Write the events in order. Think about time words or phrases that you might use to introduce these events.

....

....

....

THE ENDING

The last sentence or two usually refers back to the topic sentence. This sentence concludes, or ends, the narrative. In a narrative paragraph, the conclusion often gives the solution or tells the message or lesson that was learned.

In this example, notice how the concluding sentence refers back to the topic sentence. Also notice that it includes the lesson the person learned.

Topic sentence:

I believe that too much <u>competition</u> is not good for you.

Concluding sentence:

From this experience, **I learned that the most important person to <u>compete</u> with is myself.**

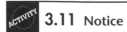 **3.11** Notice

Read the concluding sentences from some of the paragraphs in this unit. What did the person learn from each experience? Underline it.

1 When she took her first step on her new, prosthetic foot, her smile was like sunshine. She knew she could dance again.

2 One of the most important things we did was change our attitude. I say my dad saved my life, but he says I saved his, too.

3 On that hike, we learned the importance of following directions.

 3.12 Write Topic and Concluding Sentences

Write a good topic sentence and concluding sentence for the paragraph below. Discuss your choice with a partner.

WRITING PROMPT: Sometimes you do the right things for the wrong reasons. Tell the story of one time you thought this.

I never thought much about exercise. I believed in moderation in all things, including exercise. I thought, "Some exercise is good. *Too* much is bad." However, one day a beautiful young woman walked into my communication class. Her name was Jana. I wanted her to notice me. I wanted to have big muscles. I started going to the gym every day. I exercised a lot. After a while, I looked like Superman. However, Jana still did not notice me. Then one day, a group of students went for coffee after class. Jana was with us. We were walking on the sidewalk. There was a lot of traffic. Suddenly, a car lost control. It came up on the sidewalk and crashed. Jana was under the front wheel of the car! She screamed. She could not move. I took off my jacket fast. Then I lifted up the car. The other students pulled her out. "My hero!" she said to me. We got married two months later.

 3.13 Apply It to Your Writing

Work with a partner. Write a concluding sentence that answers the prompt on page 75. You might use this sentence later.

A Writing Skill 1: Complex Sentences

Good writers use a variety of sentences in their writing to make the ideas more interesting to read and easier to understand. It's important for writers to understand different sentence types so they can include a mix of sentences.

A **complex sentence** has two clauses. One is the main clause, or **independent clause**. The other is the **dependent clause**. A **subordinating conjunction**, such as *when* or *because*, begins the dependent clause. The dependent clause can come first or second in a sentence. Add a comma after the dependent clause when it comes first in the sentence

INDEPENDENT CLAUSE   DEPENDENT CLAUSE

*Timo came home for a nap **after** he finished the exam.*

DEPENDENT CLAUSE   INDEPENDENT CLAUSE

***After** he finished the exam, Timo came home for a nap.*

TYPES OF COMPLEX SENTENCES

1 **Time clauses** show the order of events in a sentence. Use subordinators such as *when*, *before*, and *after* to show the order of events in the sentence. Use *when* to refer to the time that something started.	FIRST EVENT SECOND EVENT *You should not drink coffee **before** you go to bed.* ***When** she finished her exam, she celebrated with her friends.*
2 **Reason clauses** answer the question, *Why?* They show the cause and effect of two events. Use *because* with the dependent clause (the cause).	CAUSE EFFECT **Because** Jay had an exam, he stayed up late to study. EFFECT CAUSE *Students are tired **because** they do not get enough sleep.*
3 **Conditional clauses** describe possible situations in the present or future.	*If you get enough sleep, it helps you to remember information.* *You will have more energy **if** you get a good night's sleep.*

ACTIVITY **4.1** Combine Sentences with *Because*

For each pair of sentences, choose the one that is the cause. Then combine the sentences in two ways. Use *because* in both ways.

1 a Lili never had much time in the morning.

  b Lili had just coffee for breakfast.

....

....

2 a Lili soon felt hungry and had no energy.

  b Lili did not have a nutritious breakfast.

....

....

....

3 a Lili decided to have a complete breakfast every morning.

  b Lili's work was suffering.

....

....

....

4 a There was a significant improvement in her energy each day.

  b She began the day with a good breakfast.

....

....

....

4.2 Combine Sentences

Combine each pair of sentences with a subordinator.

1 *when*

   First event: A new diet trend appears.

   Second event: People get very excited.

   ....

   ....

2 *before*

   First event: There were the "low-fat diets" of the 1980s.

   Second event: The "low-sugar diets" of today appeared.

   ....

   ....

3 *after*

   First event: A movie star recommends a diet trend.

   Second event: Many people change what they eat.

   ....

   ....

Ⓑ Writing Skill 2: Avoiding Sentence Fragments

Sentence fragments are common mistakes in writing. A fragment is a sentence that is missing something essential, such as a subject or a verb. If it begins with a capital letter and ends with a period, it *looks* like a sentence but, it is not a **complete** sentence if these elements are missing.

AVOIDING SENTENCE FRAGMENTS	
1 Make sure that a sentence has a subject and a verb.	**It makes** *Sleep is important for good health. ~~Makes~~ the brain ready for the next day.* (missing subject) **am** *I never get enough sleep. I tired all the time.* (missing verb)
2 Make sure that a sentence with a subordinator has two clauses.	**when** *I'm going to the gym. ~~When~~ I finish this homework.* **because** *Niko is tired. ~~Because~~ he got only four hours of sleep last night.*

Underline six sentence fragments in the paragraph below. On a separate sheet of paper, rewrite the paragraph to correct the fragments.

An Amazing Experience

On my grandmother's 65th birthday, she had an amazing experience. She and two friends went to a nice restaurant for her birthday. They sat down. Ordered fish, vegetables, and a glass of wine. Then they noticed a man and his wife at a table near them. The man Jack LaLanne! The three ladies went to his table. "Excuse me," my grandmother said, "but I want to thank you. You and your TV program changed my life. When I was young." Jack LaLanne smiled. His wife smiled and said, "He's *still* young! He 92 years old." Jack LaLanne looked wonderful. He said to my grandmother, "If you want to stay healthy always. You must remember two things. Exercise is king! Good food is queen!" Four years later, we all heard the sad news. Jack LaLanne died at age 96. It a good, long life. He changed a lot of lives. My grandmother will never forget the day she met him.

C Grammar for Writing: Pronouns

Pronouns are words that take the place of nouns or refer to nouns. Writers use pronouns to avoid repeating the noun too often and to make their writing flow more smoothly.

TYPES OF PRONOUNS

Subject	Object	Possessive Determiner + Noun	Possessive	Reflexive	Reciprocal
I	me	my + noun	mine	myself	
you	you	your + noun	yours	yourself	
he	him	his + noun	his	himself	
she	her	her + noun	hers	herself	each other
it	it	its + noun	--	itself	one another
we	us	our + noun	ours	ourselves	
they	them	their + noun	theirs	themselves	

USING PRONOUNS

1	Subject pronouns take the place of a subject.	*Alex started his diet by cutting down on junk food. First, **he** stopped drinking soda.*
2	Object pronouns take the place of an object.	***I** hate to exercise at the gym. It drives **me** crazy, but **I** know it's good for **me**.*
3	Possessive determiners take the place of possessive nouns.	*Mei's recipe is more popular than **John's**. **His** recipe is too complicated.*
4	Possessive pronouns take the place of a possessive determiner + noun.	*Did **you** bring **your** lunch today? I forgot **mine**.* *(mine = my lunch)*
5	Reflexive pronouns are in the object position when the object is the same as the subject.	***We** hurt **ourselves** on that long hike.*
6	Reciprocal pronouns show that two or more people give and receive the same action.	***Maya and Sam** help **one another** in their exercise program.* *(= Maya helps Sam, and Sam helps Maya.)*

Fill in the blanks with the correct pronouns or possessive determiners.

1   Some of my classmates do not worry about .... health.

Right now, ... just want to have a good time and enjoy

....

2   We are a team of athletes. .... commit ....

to daily exercise, but .... also believe that nutrition and sleep are

important to .... health. We rely on .... during

a race, so being fit is important.

3   Maria walks three miles a day and works in .... garden on weekends.

.... grows .... own tomatoes, carrots, broccoli,

and strawberries.

4   John tries to eat well, but sometimes .... eats junk food because

.... is fast and easy. .... takes multi-vitamin

pills every day. .... give him the vitamins that are not in

.... diet.

Avoiding Common Mistakes

Research tells us that these are the most common mistakes that students make when using
pronouns in academic writing.

> 1   **Do not use a pronoun after a noun subject.**
>
>   *My father ~~he~~ saved my life.*
>
> 2   **Remember to use a pronoun as the subject in subordinating clauses when it refers
>   to a noun in the main clause.**
>
>   he
>   *Jason stayed up late to study because ‸ had an exam the next day.*
>
> 3   **Remember to use a possessive determiner—not *the*—when talking about things
>   that are related or belong to someone.**
>
>   his
>   *He hurt ~~the~~ ‸ arm.*

Find and correct six more mistakes in the paragraph below.

Recently, my grandmother ~~she~~ decided not to pay attention to medical science. When she was young, she read all the new health studies. At that time, she learned that fat was bad for us. That's why she started to buy only nonfat milk and low-fat cheese. However, a few months ago, she read about a new study. This study it said that fat is *not* a problem. Instead, *sugar* is the big problem. When she was young, coffee and chocolate were "bad." Now both are good. Then there was research about calcium. For many years, my grandmother took a calcium pill every day for the bones because doctors they said it was important. Now they say to get calcium from food only – not a pill. Thirty years ago, her husband hurt the back. Doctors told him to stay in bed and

rest. Later, doctors told him the same thing after had a heart attack. These days, doctors say to get up and move. My grandmother is furious. Last week, she went to see her doctor. In a shopping bag, she had many magazines with articles about health. Now my grandmother does not pay attention to medical news because changes all the time. These days, she eats anything she wants and waits for medical science to change its mind.

ⓓ Avoiding Plagiarism

You usually need to say where you found your information in your writing, but sometimes you don't.

> My class read an article on happiness and success. The author included research on the topic. She showed where she got her information. My instructor said we should do the same thing. We should always say where we found our information. I'm confused, though. Sometimes, the author didn't include that information. For example, she mentions some basic facts about Mahatma Gandhi's life, but she doesn't say where she got her information. Please help!
> – Niko

Dear Niko,

The example you give is a good one. Mahatma Gandhi is a well-known leader. When we write about things or people that most people know, it's not necessary to say where you found the information about them. It's called common knowledge. The author you mention also included information from someone else's research. That's not common knowledge, so she says where she found it. You should do the same in your writing.

Good luck, Niko!

Professor Wright

WHAT IS COMMON KNOWLEDGE?

Common knowledge is information that:

- most people already know.
- you can easily find in many different places: books, magazines, websites, reference books.

COMMON KNOWLEDGE	EXAMPLES
Common scientific facts	*Polio was once a common disease throughout the world.*
Well-known people or historical events	*In the U.S.A., Jonas Salk developed the polio vaccine in 1952.*

You do not include the name of the writer or place where you find common knowledge information.

NOT COMMON KNOWLEDGE	EXAMPLES
Data, research, or information you learned in your research	*Ninety other countries began to use the polio vaccine within 10 years.*
An idea or opinion from others	*Albert Sabin, another polio researcher, disagreed with some of Jonas Salk's research.*

You must always include the name of the writer or place where you find information that is not common knowledge.

ACTIVITY 4.6 Practice

Check (✓) the sentences that are common knowledge.

1 The U.S. Civil War was a fight between the North and the South.

2 The largest mammal in the world is the blue whale.

3 Memorizing words is not a good way to learn English.

4 Harvard has almost 52,000 alumni in over 200 countries.

5 Muhammad Ali was one of the world's great heavyweight boxing champions.

In this section, you will follow the writing process to complete the final draft of your paragraph.

STEP 1: BRAINSTORM
Work with a partner. Follow the steps below to brainstorm more ideas for your topic.

1 First, read the student's brainstorm. First he developed his ideas using the freewrite in Section 1, on page 74. Then, he organized these ideas into chronological order and placed them in a timeline. What did the student change or take out? Why? Is the order of ideas clearer in the freewrite than on the timeline? Discuss this with a partner.

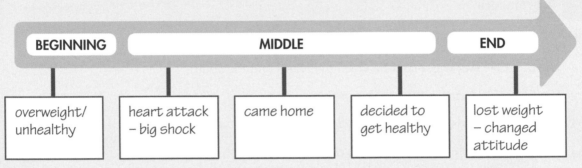

BEGINNING	MIDDLE			END
overweight/ unhealthy	heart attack – big shock	came home	decided to get healthy	lost weight – changed attitude

2 Now read your writing prompt again. Then review the ideas that you brainstormed in Section 1, page 75. Write the best ones in the timeline below. Include ideas from the Your Turns throughout the unit. Finally, brainstorm more ideas. You will probably not use every idea, but it is good to write as many ideas as possible.

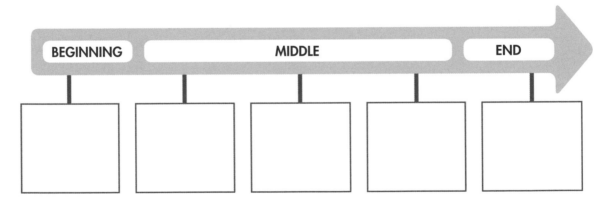

BEGINNING	MIDDLE			END

STEP 2: MAKE AN OUTLINE

Complete the outline below with ideas for your paragraph from Step 1.

PARAGRAPH OUTLINE

Topic Sentence	
Beginning	A.
Detail	1.
Middle	B.
Detail	1.
Middle	C.
Detail	1.
Middle	D.
Detail	1.
End	E.
Detail	1.
Concluding Sentence	

STEP 3: WRITE YOUR FIRST DRAFT

Now it is time to write your first draft. Here are some suggestions on how to get started.

1 Use your outline and the sentences you wrote in the Your Turns and in Step 2 on page 99.

2 Focus on making your ideas as clear as possible.

3 Remember to add a title.

After you finish, read your paragraph and check for basic errors.

1 Check that all sentences have subjects and verbs.

2 Go through and look at every comma. Is it correct? Should it be a period?

3 Check that you have used a comma after adverb clauses when they start a sentence.

4 Make sure your topic sentence and supporting sentences are clear.

STEP 4: WRITE YOUR FINAL DRAFT

1 After you receive feedback on your first draft, review it carefully. Fix any errors.

2 Make a note of errors that were most frequent (misspellings, using commas instead of periods, missing verbs). Try to avoid them as you write.

3 Review the Academic Vocabulary and Academic Collocations from this unit. Are there any that you can add to your paragraph?

4 Turn to page 239 and use the Self-Editing Review to check your work one more time.

5 Write your final draft and hand it in.

4 PROCESS PARAGRAPHS

BUSINESS: GETTING AHEAD

"Believe you can and you're halfway there."

Theodore Roosevelt
(1858–1919)

About the Author:

Theodore Roosevelt was the 26th president of the United States.

Work with a partner. Read the quotation about achieving your goals. Then answer the questions.

1 The author is writing about the importance of having confidence in achieving your goals. What does he mean by saying that "you're halfway there"?

2 How important do you think confidence is in achieving your goals?

Ⓐ Connect to Academic Writing

In this unit, you will learn skills to help you write about a process. This includes describing the series of steps needed to do or achieve something. Many of these skills you already use in your daily life. You might explain to a taxi driver how to get to your home. You might tell a classmate how to order a textbook online. Or you might describe to a friend how to use a new app on their smartphone.

Ⓑ Reflect on the Topic

In this section, you will look at a writing prompt and reflect on it. Throughout the unit, you will develop ideas about this prompt. You will use these ideas to practice skills that are necessary to write your paragraph.

The writing prompt below was used for the Student Model paragraph on page 108. The student reflected on her topic and used a process diagram. This helped her plan what she would write.

WRITING PROMPT: Describe how to complete a transaction in a business setting. For example, describe how to make a sale in an electronics store. Include detailed steps and clear examples.

How to Make a Sale

approach customer

⬇

let customer know your role

⬇

explain important features of product

⬇

find out customer's needs

⬇

mention sales

⬇

be available for questions

⬇

bring customer to check-out counter

ACTIVITY 1.1 Notice

Work with a partner. Do you agree with the steps? Would you reorder any? Would you add any? Would you remove any? Share your ideas with the class.

1.2 Apply It to Your Writing

Read the prompt and follow the directions below.

WRITING PROMPT: Choose a task someone in a particular job does and describe the steps to complete it. For example, describe how to take a customer's order as a waiter, or how to take someone's temperature as a nurse. Include detailed instructions and clear examples.

1 Think of different jobs you know. They might be jobs you have done or jobs that friends or family members have done. Then choose one.

2 Think about some common tasks for the job. Then choose one and complete the title below.

3 List the steps in the process diagram that are needed to complete it. Do not worry if you have some steps out of order, or if you have too many or too few steps.

4 Compare process diagrams with a partner.

How to ....

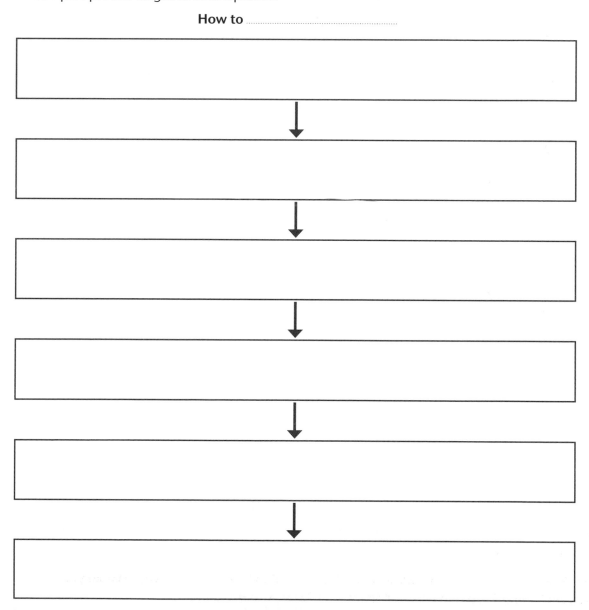

In this section, you will learn academic language that you can use in your process paragraph. You will also notice how a professional writer uses this language.

Ⓐ Academic Vocabulary

The words below appear throughout the unit. They are from the Academic Word List or the General Service List. Using these words in your writing will make your ideas clearer and your writing more academic.

key (adj)	obvious (adj)	positive (adj)	role (n)
meeting (n)	opportunity (n)	responsible (adj)	social (adj)

 2.1 Focus on Meaning

A Work with a partner. Match the words in bold to the correct definitions. Write the letters.

.... 1 The marketing manager's **role** is to create a plan to sell a product or service.

   a having the job or duty of taking care of someone or something else

.... 2 The marketing manager is a **positive** person. She always finds good things to say about her work.

   b favorable or useful

.... 3 A facilities manager is **responsible** for making sure the office runs smoothly.

   c a gathering of people for a particular purpose

.... 4 The directors' **meeting** will be next Wednesday at 2:00 in conference room 3.

   d the part someone has in a particular activity or job

B Choose the correct definitions. Write the letters.

1 His boss left the company, so he had an **opportunity** for promotion. **Opportunity** means .... for personal gain.

   a time   b possibility

2 A **key** characteristic of a successful company is having happy employees. **Key** means ....

   a necessary   b unknown

3 Many companies have **social** activities like picnics for employees and their families outside of the office. **Social** means ....

   a related to work   b related to people

4 It is **obvious** that Marta loves her job. She is always smiling and never complains. **Obvious** means ....

   a lucky   b clear

B Academic Phrases

Research tells us that the phrases in bold below are commonly used in academic writing.

> **ACTIVITY** **2.2** Focus on Meaning

Work with a partner. Read the sentences about someone trying to fix a paper jam in a photocopier. Choose the sentence that is closest in meaning to the first.

1 **The first step** is to see where the paper is stuck.

   a The best thing to do is to see where the paper is stuck.

   b Seeing where the paper is stuck is the place to start.

   c There are many steps to do to see where the paper is stuck.

2 Turn off the copier **in order to** avoid getting an electric shock.

   a Turn off the copier after you avoid getting an electric shock.

   b Turn off the copier so that you avoid getting an electric shock.

   c Turn off the copier but avoid getting an electric shock.

3 **The process of** fixing a paper jam is easy.

   a The reason that we are fixing a paper jam is easy.

   b The effects of fixing a paper jam are easy.

   c The series of steps for fixing a paper jam is easy.

C Writing in the Real World

You will read an article titled "From Receptionist to CEO." The author of the article describes the steps a receptionist took in her career.

Before you read, answer this question: How can someone rise from the bottom of a company to become the leader?

Now read the article. Think about your answer to the question as you read.

From RECEPTIONIST to CEO

by Mark Narita

1 It's not easy to get ahead in the business world. Then how did Karen Kaplan go from a receptionist **responsible** for answering the phone to CEO of Hill Holliday — one of the most successful advertising agencies[1] today? Her story begins more than 30 years ago.

2 Kaplan had no business experience when she began working at Hill Holliday. The 22-year-old had no office skills, but got a job as a receptionist. In her first week, two colleagues told her she was at the bottom of the company. "We'll see about that," recalls Kaplan.

3 How did Kaplan get ahead with no formal business education? First, she took her job very seriously and did the best she could. Second, she had excellent **social** skills. She was a good communicator and got along well with everyone at work. As people waited for **meetings**, she chatted, asked questions, and remembered **key** details about them. She kept every business card she ever received. Third, she stayed with the company long after others moved on.[2]

4 Soon, **opportunities** opened up for Kaplan. She got a promotion in another department of the company. The job came with more responsibility, including preparing a weekly report. Kaplan came in every Saturday to type the report so no one would see how long it took her. Then she came in on Sunday in order to photocopy it. One weekend, after fixing a paper jam, she found a piece of paper inside the copier with everyone's salary[3] on it. She was shocked at the high salaries of some people. She thought, "Wow, I could spend some time at this place!"

[1] **advertising agency:** a company that makes advertisements

[2] **move on:** leave a place to go somewhere else
[3] **salary:** money that someone is paid for a job

5 Kaplan was patient and stayed positive. She became an account manager and later took on the **role** of director. She jokes, "I had the same 12 jobs that everyone has. I've just had them all at Hill Holliday."

6 When Hill Holliday was in the process of selecting their next CEO, the choice was an **obvious** one. As one former CEO stated, "She was born to be CEO."

7 "You can make your mark[4] in every single job," Kaplan says. "I still run into people today who remember me from when I was a receptionist who say, 'You were the best ... receptionist in the history of receptionists.'"

[4] **make your mark:** attract recognition

 2.3 Check Your Understanding

Discuss your answers to the questions below with a partner.

1 What did Karen Kaplan do as a receptionist?

2 To get ahead in business, which pieces of advice do you think Kaplan would say are very important? Check (✓) the two best statements.

    a Get a formal education.

    b Be friendly, social, and confident.

    c Change companies every few years.

    d Do not do things you think you cannot do.

    e Remember key details about people.

    f Be realistic about what you can achieve and know your limits.

3 What do you think is important to get ahead in business these days? For example, do you think it's important to stay with the same company, or is it better to change jobs every few years? Why?

 2.4 Notice the Features of Process Writing

Answer the questions.

1 Look at some of the steps Kaplan took to get ahead. Number them from 1 to 6 in the order they happened.

    a She took on the role of director.

    b She got promoted to a job in another department.

    c She became an account manager.

    d She worked hard and got along with everyone.

    e She got a job as a receptionist.

    f She took on more responsibility, such as preparing reports.

2 Of the things Kaplan did to get ahead, which do you think was most important? Why?

In Section 1, you saw how the writer of the Student Model reflected on her topic. In this section, you will analyze the final draft of her paragraph. You will learn how to develop ideas for your own paragraph.

Ⓐ Student Model

Read the prompt and answer the questions.

WRITING PROMPT: Describe how to complete a transaction in a business setting. For example, describe how to make a sale in an electronics store. Include detailed steps and clear examples.

1 Look at the title below. How do you think the writer describes how to make a sale?

2 What steps do you think the writer will mention?

Read the paragraph twice. The first time, think about your answers to the questions above. The second time, answer the questions in the Analyze Writing Skills boxes. This will help you notice key features of a process paragraph.

Making a Sale

The process of making a sale is easy if you follow these five steps. This is based on my experience working at an electronic appliance store. The first step is to approach the customer and let them know your **role**. Tell them your name and position, and remember to smile. Second, find out about the customer's needs. You can do this by asking questions, such as, "Are you looking for anything special today?" Stay close to customers who say they are "just looking." You can then be ready to help them. Next, explain the **key** features of the product. For example, a customer who is looking at headphones might want to know about the headphone's weight, design, and price. After that, be available for questions. Obviously, you are **responsible** for answering your customer's questions correctly and honestly. Finally, bring the customer to the check-out counter when you think he is ready. This is also a good time to suggest anything related to the sale. For example, I suggest things like a memory card for a camera, or a case for a laptop. Most of these steps are the same if you work in a department store, an electronics store, or a car dealership. Good salespeople follow these steps and often make a sale.

> **1 Analyze Writing Skills**
> Find the sentence that contains step 1. Write "1" over the academic phrase that begins this sentence.

> **2 Analyze Writing Skills**
> Circle the purpose of this sentence:
> a to offer en explanation
> b to give a reason
> c to give a reminder

> **3 Analyze Writing Skills**
> Find sentences that contain steps 2–5. Write 2, 3, 4, and 5 over the word that begins each sentence. Then circle the verbs that tell the reader to do certain things.

Answer the questions.

1 What five steps does the writer suggest for making a sale? Do you think they are all necessary? What steps, if any, would you add?

2 The writer claims that "most of these steps are the same if you work in a department store, an electronics store, or a car dealership." Do you think that's true? Why or why not?

3 How would you react if a salesperson used these five steps to try and sell you something?

ACTIVITY **3.2** Outline the Writer's Ideas

Complete the outline for "Making a Sale." Use the phrases in the box.

an opportunity to sell more	be available for questions
explain product's key features	find out about needs by asking questions
remember to smile	stay nearby customers who are "just looking"

PARAGRAPH OUTLINE

1st Step   A. Approach customer, let them know your role

Detail   1.

2nd Step   B.

Detail   1. "Are you looking for anything special today?"

Detail   2.

3rd Step   C.

Detail   1. For headphone – weight, design, price

4th Step   D.

Detail   1. Responsibility to be honest

5th Step   E. Ask customer if ready to check out

Detail   1.

B Process Paragraphs

Process paragraphs are sometimes called **"how to"** paragraphs. They explain how to do or achieve something. When writing about a process, writers list the steps and add support to each step so the reader understands exactly what to do. The steps should be clear and easy for the reader to follow.

Read the two paragraphs below. Which paragraph has steps that are easier to follow?

Paragraph 1

Steps to Becoming a Chef

It's important to have a clear plan in place if you want a career in the culinary arts. Get a part-time job in the field. Learn all you can while trying to get noticed by people in the field. Apply to a culinary arts school. Think about what exactly you want to do in the field of culinary arts. You might work in a restaurant, a school, a hospital, a cruise ship, or even work as a private chef. Follow these steps and you can start your career in the culinary arts.

Paragraph 2

Steps to Becoming a Chef

It's important to have a clear plan in place if you want a career in the culinary arts. First, get a part-time job in the field. For example, get work as a cook or as an assistant to a chef. After that, learn all you can while trying to get noticed by people in the field. You can do this by letting others know you are interested in a professional career in the culinary arts. Next, apply to a culinary arts school. Finally, think about exactly what you want to do in the field of culinary arts. You might work in a restaurant, a school, a hospital, a cruise ship, or even work as a private chef. Follow these steps and you can start your career in the culinary arts.

It is clear that paragraph 2 is easier to follow. Why? It's because the steps are introduced with words like *First, Then, Next*, and *After that*. These words signal a new step is to follow. The steps are also well supported with details.

TOPIC SENTENCES AND CONTROLLING IDEAS

Like other types of paragraphs, a process paragraph needs a **topic sentence**. The topic sentence includes the **topic** and its **controlling idea**. The **controlling idea** tells the process that the reader will read about. It often expresses an opinion or attitude about the process. It might say, for example, how clear, easy, or important the process is.

A topic sentence in a process paragraph often uses the word "process" or "steps" – not "things" – to make it clear to the reader that a series of steps follows. The topic sentence does not always say exactly how many steps are in the process, but when it does, it provides additional support for the reader as he or she reads through the steps.

Imagine students are given the following writing prompt: *Describe how to attract new customers to a neighborhood coffee shop you know.* Look at why sentence 1 is not a very good topic sentence.

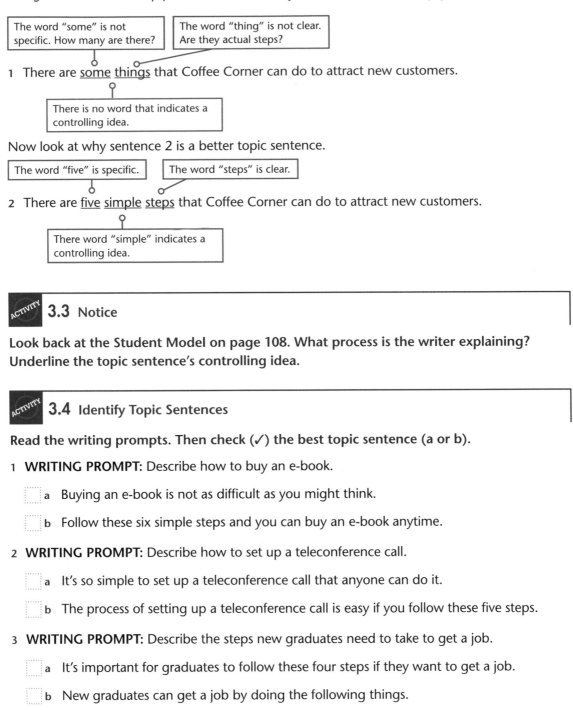

| The word "some" is not specific. How many are there? | The word "thing" is not clear. Are they actual steps? |

1 There are <u>some</u> <u>things</u> that Coffee Corner can do to attract new customers.

There is no word that indicates a controlling idea.

Now look at why sentence 2 is a better topic sentence.

| The word "five" is specific. | The word "steps" is clear. |

2 There are <u>five</u> <u>simple</u> <u>steps</u> that Coffee Corner can do to attract new customers.

There word "simple" indicates a controlling idea.

ACTIVITY 3.3 Notice

Look back at the Student Model on page 108. What process is the writer explaining? Underline the topic sentence's controlling idea.

ACTIVITY 3.4 Identify Topic Sentences

Read the writing prompts. Then check (✓) the best topic sentence (a or b).

1 **WRITING PROMPT:** Describe how to buy an e-book.

☐ a Buying an e-book is not as difficult as you might think.

☐ b Follow these six simple steps and you can buy an e-book anytime.

2 **WRITING PROMPT:** Describe how to set up a teleconference call.

☐ a It's so simple to set up a teleconference call that anyone can do it.

☐ b The process of setting up a teleconference call is easy if you follow these five steps.

3 **WRITING PROMPT:** Describe the steps new graduates need to take to get a job.

☐ a It's important for graduates to follow these four steps if they want to get a job.

☐ b New graduates can get a job by doing the following things.

3.5 Write Topic Sentences

Look at each writing prompt. Write a topic sentence with a controlling idea.
Then compare your sentences with a partner.

1 **WRITING PROMPT**: Describe what you should do if your computer freezes.

   ....

   ....

2 **WRITING PROMPT**: What steps must someone take to get ready for a job interview?

   ....

   ....

3 **WRITING PROMPT**: Describe what an employer needs to do to give an employee a
   written warning.

   ....

   ....

4 **WRITING PROMPT**: What steps should a department store customer service representative
   take when a customer wants to return a purchase?

   ....

   ....

 3.6 Apply It to Your Writing

Work with a partner. Look at your topic and the brainstorm you completed in
Section 1 on page 103. Write possible topic sentences.

....

....

....

....

....

....

WRITING STEPS IN PROCESS PARAGRAPHS

The steps are a very important part of a process paragraph. The steps in a process paragraph need to be in **chronological** (also called **sequential**) **order**. This means they are presented in the exact order they are to be followed. This allows the reader to easily follow them.

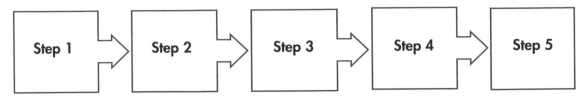

Some paragraphs may appear to describes processes but are, in fact, more like giving advice. In cases like this, the writer may suggest that the reader do certain things, but the order is not particularly important. It is therefore not a true process. A paragraph titled "How to Be a Team Player," for example, will only be a process paragraph if the steps are in a chronological order, and dependent on one another. It will not be a process paragraph if it just lists advice in an order that is not chronological.

You can check if a paragraph is a process paragraph by putting the steps in a different order. If you did this with a process paragraph, the paragraph would quickly no longer make sense.

Writers usually help the reader identify the steps by using the following **transition words and phrases**:

First step: *First, Firstly, The first step is, … First of all, …*

Later steps: *Second, Third, and Fourth, Next, Then, After that,*

Final step: *Finally, Lastly, The final step is …*

You will learn more about these words and phrases in Section 4.

A writer does not usually only list the steps. He or she also adds supporting sentences after some or all of the steps. These may include examples, explanations, or other types of support the writer thinks will help make the steps clearer and easier to follow.

 3.7 Notice

Look back at Paragraph 2 on page 111. Write the four steps.

Step 1: ....

Step 2: ....

Step 3: ....

Step 4: ....

3.8 Write Steps

Add these steps to the correct place in the paragraph below. Write the letters.

a click the upload button

b give your video a title and description

c open the video

d press the Share button

e tag the video

How to Upload a Video

You can publish a video from your smartphone in just five quick steps. First, ... After the video is open, ... You may have several choices, so select where you want to share the video.
(1)
(2)
Next, ... This lets people quickly understand the content of your video. After that, ...
(3)
(4)
This includes information about who is in the video. Finally, ... Now the video is available for others to see, and possibly share themselves. If you follow these steps, you can upload any video in very little time.
(5)

 3.9 Order Steps

The steps below are from a paragraph titled "How to Order a Book Online." First put the steps on the left in the correct order. Then match each step to a detail on the right.

.... Click on the book you want to order.

.... Put in your credit card details and click "purchase."

.... Choose the website with the best price.

.... Add your personal information.

...1... Compare the price of the book on different websites.

.... a For example, this could include your name, age, and address.

...1... b Prices can vary a great deal from site to site.

.... c It may go into an area called "shopping cart."

.... d It's a good idea to wait until you get verification that the purchase went through.

.... e You may even want to bookmark the site for future reference.

3.10 Write Details

Work with a partner. Use your own ideas to write details to complete the paragraph.

Getting a Job Interview in Five Steps

Getting a job interview is never easy, but following these simple steps will make it easier.
First, decide what kind of job you want. ....
.... (1) ....

Second, start researching companies you want to work for. ....
.... (2) ....

Next, prepare your résumé. ....
.... (3) ....

After that, send out your résumé to all the companies you want to interview with. ....
.... (4) ....

Finally, search for other jobs through social media, recruitment fairs, and friends. ....
.... (5) ....

It is obviously good to keep searching for other jobs while you wait. These steps are not difficult and, in time, they will help you get that job interview.

3.11 Apply It to Your Writing

Work with a partner. Choose one step you listed in Section 1 on page 103 and write a sentence that supports it using a reason, an explanation, or an example.

....

....

CONCLUDING SENTENCES

Like other paragraphs, process paragraphs have a **concluding sentence**. This sentence mentions the process again, and the controlling idea from the topic sentence is often expressed in another way. Notice in the example below how the controlling idea of "quick" in the topic sentence is expressed in the concluding sentence as "in very little time."

Topic sentence: *You can publish a video from your smartphone in just five quick steps.*

Concluding sentence: *If you follow these steps, you can upload any video in very little time.*

 3.12 Notice

Look back at Activity 3.10 on page 116. Underline the concluding sentence. Then circle the controlling idea that is similar to the one in the topic sentence.

 3.13 Practice Writing

A **Work with a partner. Read the writing prompt. Decide on and write the steps. Add more steps if necessary.**

WRITING PROMPT: Describe the steps someone needs to follow to have a productive business meeting. Think about what someone needs to do first, second, third, etc.

First, ...

....

Second, ...

....

After that, ...

....

Next, ...

....

Finally, ...

....

B With your partner, to complete the paragraph. Include the steps from Part A on page 117 and any additional details you think are important.

It's important to follow these steps to have a productive business meeting.

....

....

....

....

....

....

....

....

....

....

....

In sum, follow these steps and you will soon have a good business meeting.

C Exchange your work with another pair. Read their paragraph. Do you have similar steps?

ACTIVITY **3.14** Apply It to Your Writing

YOUR
TURN

Look back at your topic sentence in Activity 3.6 on page 113 and write a possible concluding sentence for your paragraph.

....

....

....

....

Ⓐ Writing Skill 1: Transitions of Sequential Order

Good writers help their readers follow the various steps in the process they are describing. They use certain words and phrases, called **transitions**, that signal the introduction of a new step. These transitions are similar to the ones used for chronological order. After all of these transition words, a comma (,) is required.

TRANSITIONS OF SEQUENTIAL ORDER	
1 A writer often indicates the first step in a process by saying *First* or *First of all*.	*First*, look at the screen to see where the paper is stuck.
2 The writer may choose to indicate each step with a number, such as *Second*, *Third*, and *Fourth*. These are used when there are only a few steps in the process.	*First*, look at the screen to see where the paper is stuck. **Second**, open the part of the printer where the paper is. **Third**, gently pull the paper from the copier. **Fourth**, close the part of the printer where the paper was.
3 Another way the writer can indicate each step is by saying *Next, Then,* and *After that*. These can be repeated and all mean the same thing.	*First*, look at the screen to see where the paper is stuck. **Next**, open the part of the printer where the paper is. **Then**, gently pull the paper from the copier. **After that**, close the part of the printer where the paper was.
4 The writer can indicate the final step by saying *Finally* or *Lastly*.	**Finally**, give time for the printer to warm back up.

ACTIVITY 4.1 Write Transitions

Complete the paragraph using the transition words below. More than one answer may be possible.

after that	first of all	lastly	next	then

How to Fill a Photocopier

It's very simple to fill a photocopier with paper. .... (1) , find the drawer in the copier that holds the paper. .... (2) , gently pull out the drawer. .... (3) , open a packet of paper and run your thumb along the edges. This helps separate the paper so it does not stick together later. .... (4) , place the paper inside the drawer and make sure it's in place. .... (5) , close the drawer. Now you're ready to copy again with new paper.

B Writing Skill 2: Adding Details

Writers often need to explain each step so that the reader understands how to complete it. It's also important that they include the right amount of detail. With too little detail the reader may not have enough information to complete the task. With too much detail, the reader may get lost and be unable to follow the steps.

As you learned in Unit 1, good writers include specific **examples, explanations, and reasons** in their paragraphs. For process paragraphs, it is also useful to include the following details:

ADDING DETAILS	
1 A **reminder** provides additional information and can help break up a series of steps. Don't confuse reminders with steps.	STEP *Second, find out about the customer's needs.* REMINDER **Remember to smile and ask questions.**
2 A **warning** makes clear what *not* to do	STEP *Second, find out about the customer's needs.* WARNING **Do not ask questions that are too direct or personal.**
3 Do not include details that are **irrelevant** or not important. They can easily distract the reader.	*Second, find out about the customer's needs.* ~~I need to buy a gift for my brother.~~

 4.2 Write Details

Read the paragraph below. Use the ideas below to add details to make the steps clearer. Rewrite the paragraph on a separate piece of paper.

1 Add an explanation to make "home office" clearer.

2 Add a reminder about places in the home that may not be appropriate for a home office.

3 Add an example for how you might organize your desk.

4 Add a reason for why it is important to have a clean work area.

5 Add a warning to others regarding your office hours.

How to Set Up a Home Office

It is very easy to set up a home office these days. First, find a place in your home that will be used for a home office and nothing else. Next, clean the area and remove anything you will not need for your office. Then, buy some office furniture and arrange it in the clean space. After that, organize your desk. Finally, set your office hours and let people know what they are. You now have an office space that was easy to create.

C Grammar for Writing: Imperatives

The **imperative** is widely used in English to give advice or instructions, or to express requests or commands. Study these rules:

IMPERATIVES	
1 The imperative uses the base form of the verb.	*Remember to smile.* *Be available for questions.*
2 In imperative sentences, the subject is a singular or plural *you*. Don't write *you*, because it is understood.	*Enjoy yourself.* *Enjoy yourselves.*
3 Use *Do not* + the base verb for negative commands. *Do not* is often contracted to *Don't*.	*Do not bother the customer.* *Do not forget to thank the customer.*
4 You can begin imperatives with *always* and *never*.	*Always be friendly and polite.* *Never ask personal questions.*
5 You can use the imperative with time clauses. Include the pronoun *you* after words like *If* and *When*.	*If you answer the questions, answer them honestly.* *Bring customers to the check-out counter **when** you think they are ready.*

 4.3 Write Imperatives

Complete the paragraph with the correct verbs. If necessary, make the verb negative.

brainstorm	choose	forget	get	look at	remember	remove	test

How to Choose a Name for a New Business

Choosing a name for your new business may sound like a challenge, but it can be easy – and fun – if you follow these steps. First of all, ... a group of people
(1)
together. They can be people who are starting the business, or friends, or even strangers. Then .... possible names. This means you just say any names that
(2)
come to mind. .... to write all the names down.
(3)
Next, ... any names that are already used, are too long, or obviously
(4)
do not sound good. After that, ... your list and choose about five
(5)
that most of you like. Then .... them. For example, say them aloud or
(6)
just ask others for their opinion. Finally, ... your new business name.
(7)
.... to register your name so you know you can use it legally.
(8)
Following these steps can help you find your new business name.

Avoiding Common Mistakes

Research tells us that these are the most common mistakes that students make when using imperatives in academic writing.

> **1 Use *Do not* + base form of the verb. Do not use *no* with the base form in imperatives.**
>
> *Do not*
> ~~No~~ *forget to write down the names.*
>
> **2 Write *do not* as two words, not one.**
>
> *Do not*
> ~~Donot~~ *forget to write down the names.*
>
> **3 Use the imperative – not the simple present with *you* – to explain a process.**
>
> *If no one likes the names, ~~you~~ remove them from the list.*

 4.4 Editing Task

Find and correct four more mistakes in the paragraph below.

How to Make Coffee at Work

Anyone can make coffee in just five steps in our office
Do not
pantry. First, fill the pot with water. ~~Donot~~ fill it with hot water – always use cold water. Then, take a coffee filter, you fill it with some coffee, and place the filter and coffee into the coffee maker. Next, pour the water carefully into the coffee maker. No spill it! After that, place the empty pot on the burner under the filter and turn it on. Leave the coffee there until it is done. Finally, you enjoy your coffee. When the coffee pot is empty, donot forget to empty the filter and wash the pot for the next person. See what an easy process coffee making can be!

D Avoiding Plagiarism

Good sources are important for academic writing, but how do you find them?

We read an interesting article about businesses helping their communities. My instructor told us two things. First, the author used an excellent source for his article. Second, we should look carefully at the author's sources. I don't know what a source is. I don't understand my instructor's explanation. What is a source? Where can I find one?
– Yukiko

Dear Yukiko,

You ask good questions. A source can be a book, article, government report, or even a video. A source gives you information for your paper. This information can support your opinions and ideas, but it does not take the place of your own opinions and ideas. These days, most students find sources on the Internet. You can also use the library. Reference librarians are there to help you. Don't be afraid to ask them for help!

Best,

Professor Wright

FINDING SOURCES

There are two key places where people find sources for papers: in a library and on the Internet.

PLACES TO FIND SOURCES	SOURCES
• In a library, you can find the most resources for your research.	books scholarly journals newspapers magazines videos
• On the Internet, you can use a search engine. Choose good key search words and you will find good sources.	online magazines and newspapers online books and scholarly journals government reports podcasts audio and video

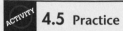 **4.5** Practice

A Read the four writing prompts below. Then read the list of key search words. Which ones will help you find good sources on the Internet? Choose two good key words for each prompt.

.... and .... 1 What can businesses do to protect the environment?

.... and .... 2 Should business schools teach ethics to their students?

.... and .... 3 How can small companies help disabled employees?

.... and .... 4 Discuss how small loans help people in developing countries.

KEY WORDS

a business school   e small loans

b businesses   f disabled employees

c developing countries   g ethics

d environment   h small companies

B Look at the prompt below. Work with a partner. Write two good key words for this topic.

Discuss how businesses can help working mothers.

.... and ....

In this section, you will follow the writing process to complete the final draft of your paragraph.

STEP 1: BRAINSTORM

Work with a partner. Follow the steps below to brainstorm more ideas for your topic.

1 First, read the student's brainstorm. She wrote many ideas from the process diagram she used to reflect on her topic in Section 1 on page 102. Which step is not included in the Student Model?

How to Make a Sale

approach customer

↓

let customer know your role

↓

explain important features of product

↓

find out customer's needs

↓

mention sales and special promotions

↓

be available for questions

↓

bring customer to check-out counter

2 Now read your writing prompt again. Then review the ideas that you brainstormed in Section 1, page 103. Write the best ones in the process diagram below. Include ideas from the Your Turns throughout the unit. Finally, brainstorm more ideas. You will probably not use every idea, but it is good to write as many ideas as possible.

How to ....

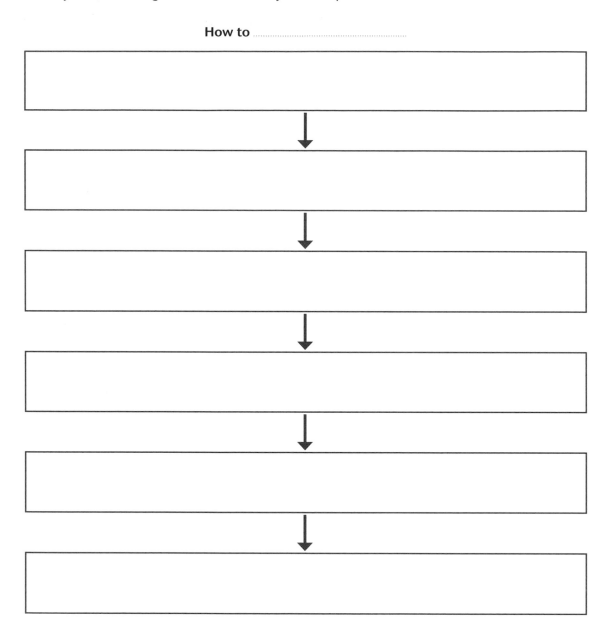

STEP 2: MAKE AN OUTLINE

Complete the outline below with ideas for your paragraph from Step 1.

PARAGRAPH OUTLINE

Topic Sentence	....
1st Step	A. ....
Detail	1. ....
Detail	2. ....
2nd Step	B. ....
Detail	1. ....
Detail	2. ....
3rd Step	C. ....
Detail	1. ....
Detail	2. ....
4th Step	D. ....
Detail	1. ....
Detail	2. ....
5th Step	E. ....
Detail	1. ....
Detail	2. ....
Concluding Sentence	....

STEP 3: WRITE YOUR FIRST DRAFT

Now it's time to write your first draft. Here are some suggestions on how to get started.

1 Use your outline and the sentences you wrote in the Your Turns and in Step 2 on page 127.

2 Focus on making your ideas as clear as possible.

3 Add a title.

After you finish, read your paragraph and check for basic errors.

1 Check that all sentences have subjects and verbs.

2 Go through and look at every comma. Is it correct? Should it be a period?

3 Check that you have used a comma after adverb clauses when they start a sentence.

4 Make sure your topic sentence and supporting sentences are clear.

STEP 4: WRITE YOUR FINAL DRAFT

1 After you receive feedback on your first draft, review it carefully. Fix any errors.

2 Make a note of errors that were most frequent (misspellings, using commas instead of periods, missing verbs). Try to avoid them as you write.

3 Review the Academic Vocabulary and Phrases from this unit. Are there any that you can add to your paragraph?

4 Turn to page 240 and use the Self-Editing Review to check your work one more time.

5 Write your final draft and hand it in.

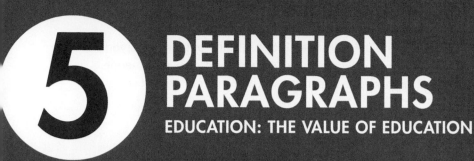

5 DEFINITION PARAGRAPHS

EDUCATION: THE VALUE OF EDUCATION

"Education is not just preparation for life, but part of life itself."

Henry Ford
(1863–1947)

About the Author:

Henry Ford was the founder of the Ford Motor Company.

Work with a partner. Read the quotation about education. Then answer the questions.

1 Why does the author say that education is "part of life itself"?

2 In what ways does education prepare a young person for life?

3 Do you think that education will always be part of your life? Why?

Ⓐ Connect to Academic Writing

In this unit, you will learn skills to help you write definition paragraphs. Many of these skills you already use in your daily life. You might define an unknown word in your language to someone who speaks a different language. Or you might define a technical term from your area of study to a friend who is unfamiliar with it.

Ⓑ Reflect on the Topic

In this section, you will look at a writing prompt and reflect on it. Throughout the unit, you will develop ideas about this prompt. You will use these ideas to practice skills that are necessary to write your paragraph.

The writing prompt below was used for the Student Model paragraph on page 136.
The student used a cluster diagram to brainstorm ideas to define what a vocational school is.

WRITING PROMPT: There are many different types of higher-education institutions. Choose an institution – high school, community college, vocational school, or university – and define it.

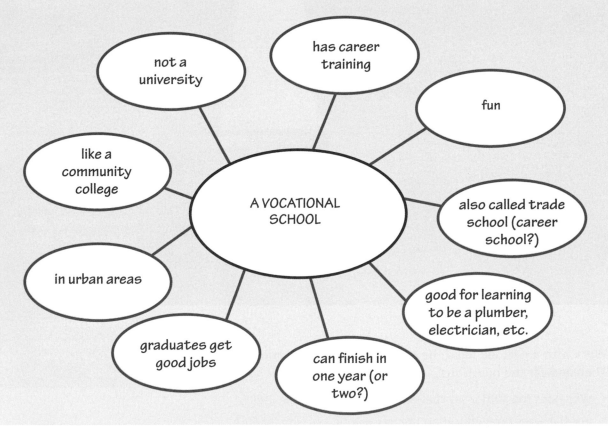

 1.1 Notice

Work with a partner. How would you define a vocational school? Add one or two additional ideas to the cluster diagram. Share your ideas with the class.

1.2 **Apply It to Your Writing**

Read the prompt and follow the directions below.

WRITING PROMPT: Success in education often requires good grades. Define a grade.

1 Think about your answers to the questions below.

- Who uses grades?
- Why do people use them?
- When do people use them?

- Who are grades important to?
- What kind of grades are there?
- What are some examples of grades?

2 Write your ideas in the cluster diagram.

3 Compare cluster diagrams with a partner.

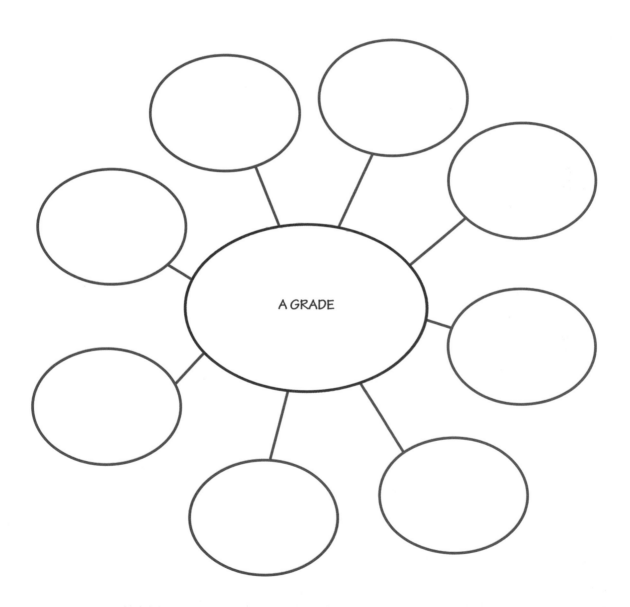

2 EXPAND YOUR KNOWLEDGE

In this section, you will learn academic language that you can use in your definition paragraph. You will also notice how a professional writer uses this language.

Ⓐ Academic Vocabulary

The words below appear throughout the unit. They are from the Academic Word List or the General Service List. Using these words in your writing will make your ideas clearer and your writing more academic.

advantage (n)	connection (n)	expect (v)	explain (v)
beneficial (adj)	education (n)	experience (n)	reward (n)

 2.1 Focus on Meaning

A Work with a partner. Complete the sentences with the correct words or phrases. Circle the letters.

1 One **advantage** of going to college is that you usually get a better paid job afterward. An **advantage** gives someone a .... chance of success.

   a greater   b lesser

2 Members of the university staff **explain** the housing rules to new students. They give presentations to these students at the start of the school year. **Explain** means to .... about something.

   a give opinions   b give information

3 He is successful because he got a good **education**. He had good teachers and studied hard. **Education** is the .... someone gets from a school, college, or university.

   a skills and knowledge   b books and articles

4 There is a **connection** between music and language because they both use the same part of the brain. **Connection** means ....

   a separation   b relationship

B Read the sentences. Match the words in bold to the correct meanings. Write the letters.

.... 1 Include your work **experience** on your résumé. This can include any part-time work, summer jobs, and volunteer work.

a helpful or useful

.... 2 As a **reward** for graduating high school, my parents bought me a car.

b to think something will happen

.... 3 I have not heard if I passed my final exam. But I **expect** to hear soon.

c knowledge that you gain from doing something

.... 4 It is **beneficial** to talk to your advisors. They can help you solve problems at college.

d something good that you get because you worked hard, behaved well, etc.

B Academic Collocations

Collocations are words that are frequently used together. Research tells us that the academic vocabulary in Part A is commonly used in the collocations in bold below.

 2.2 Focus on Meaning

Work with a partner. Read the sentences. Decide the meaning of the collocations in bold and circle the correct meaning.

1 Lower tuition fees could allow more people to go into **higher education**.

  a middle school or high school   b college or university

2 Students can find ways to save money. For example, they can **take advantage of** student discounts. At some clothing stores, students can buy some things for a cheaper price.

  a use as an opportunity   b be surprised about

3 It is **extremely beneficial** to have a laptop at college. For example, a laptop lets you take notes during lectures.

  a very easy   b very helpful

4 A volunteer job is a job that does not pay money. People do them because they can **gain experience** from them.

  a get knowledge and skills from doing something

  b get knowledge and skills from reading about something

5 There is a **close connection** between a person's level of education and his or her salary.

  a surprising result   b strong relationship

C Writing in the Real World

You will read an article titled "The Benefits of a College Education." In the article, the author defines concepts that may be unfamiliar to the reader.

Before you read, answer this question: What do you think are some of the benefits?

Now read the article. Think about your answer to the question as you read.

THE BENEFITS OF A COLLEGE EDUCATION

by Hector Ollarzabal

1   Is it worth the time, effort, and money to get a college degree? The answer is yes! First of all, one of the most obvious reasons to get a degree is to increase your salary. People who get degrees generally make more money than those who don't. According to the U.S. Census Bureau, people in the U.S.A. who only finish high school earn, on average, $32,500 a year. Those with bachelor's degrees earn $55,700. Those with master's degrees earn $63,000. Get a Ph.D. and you make $100,000 or more. Over a lifetime of working, the financial **rewards** are huge. Clearly, it's extremely **beneficial** to pursue higher **education**.

2   People with degrees also have more job opportunities. College graduates are able to complete tasks on time and think critically[1] – two qualities that employers look for. For these reasons employers want to hire[2] college graduates. A college degree allows you to work in areas a high school graduate cannot. It lets you take **advantage** of more career options by opening doors that would otherwise be closed. Going to college also provides networking opportunities that are not available to those who didn't attend college. The number of **connections** increases with every level of education.

3   People with college degrees generally have higher degrees of job satisfaction than people with a high school education. Job satisfaction is defined as how happy someone is in his or her job. How can we **explain** this? Degree holders are able to get high-paying jobs. They can also advance in a company and receive benefits. Perhaps most importantly, they gain **experience** in the fields that actually interest them. According to a recent survey from the University of Chicago, some of the most satisfying jobs are teacher, engineer, physical therapist, and office administrator. All require a college degree.

4   Jobs that require a college education lead to greater job stability. Job stability means an employee can **expect** to keep the same job for a long time. This is a key benefit when there are few jobs to be found, or when companies need to reduce their employee numbers. The first people to lose their jobs are often unskilled workers.

5   Finally, earning a degree has a positive impact on a person's communication skills. The ability to listen to others, ask the right questions, and speak with confidence[3] may just help you get the job you want.

[1] **thinking critically**: thinking carefully about something, not allowing feelings or opinions to affect you
[2] **hire**: to give someone a job

[3] **confidence**: feeling certain of your ability to do things well

 2.3 **Check Your Understanding**

Answer the questions.

1 Which of the five benefits of a college education do you think the author feels is most important? Why? What do *you* think is the main benefit of getting a college degree?

2 What are some other reasons for going to college that are not mentioned in the reading?

3 Do you think it's possible to have the benefits mentioned in the reading without getting a college degree? Explain your answer.

 2.4 **Notice the Features of Definition Writing**

Answer the questions.

1 Read the third paragraph again. What does the author define? What phrase does the writer use when defining the term?

2 Read the fourth paragraph again. What does the author define? What verb does the writer use when defining the term?

3 Find another word or phrase that you think needs to be defined in the reading. How would you define it?

In Section 1, you saw how the writer of the Student Model reflected on her topic. In this section, you will analyze the final draft of her paragraph. You will learn how to develop ideas for your own paragraph.

Ⓐ Student Model

Read the prompt and answer the questions.

WRITING PROMPT: There are many different types of higher-education insitutions. Choose an institution – high school, community college, vocational school, or university – and define it.

1 Look at the title and the photo below. What do you think a vocational school is?

2 What do you think makes vocational schools different from other types of schools?

3 What do you think students can learn in vocational schools?

Read the paragraph twice. The first time, think about your answers to the questions above. The second time, answer the questions in the Analyze Writing Skills boxes. This will help you notice the key features of a definition paragraph.

STUDENT MODEL

Vocational Schools

Vocational schools are a type of school which provide career training. They are similar to community colleges because they both offer shorter courses of study. Vocational schools are not universities. At a vocational school, students study two years or less, and they focus on a single field, such as health services, flower design, or car repair. This is an **advantage** for students who already know what they want to do. People interested in changing or finding new careers also attend vocational schools. For example, a salesperson who is unhappy at work might learn new skills at a vocational school. Also, stay-at-home mothers use vocational schools after they have raised their children. For these people, a short-term training program makes a lot of sense. Vocational schools also often have close **connections** with the businesses in the community. Students gain work **experience** at these businesses. The businesses spend time and money training students, so graduates can **expect** to get a good job there. This is extremely **beneficial** for people who want to get a job after they graduate.

> **1 Analyze Writing Skills**
> Find and underline the part of the sentence that defines "vocational schools."

> **2 Analyze Writing Skills**
> Find and underline the sentence that states what vocational schools are not.

> **3 Analyze Writing Skills**
> Find and circle the two conjunctions (e.g. *and, but, or, so*) that join two independent clauses.

> **4 Analyze Writing Skills**
> Find and circle the word *who*. Underline the rest of the sentence after *who*.

Answer the questions.

1 Explain what a vocational school is in your own words.

2 What are some advantages that vocational schools have over other types of schools?

3 Do you have vocational schools where you live? Do you think you would enjoy attending one?

3.2 Outline the Writer's Ideas

Complete the outline for "Vocational Schools." Use the phrases in the box.

focus on single field	similar to community colleges
have close connections with businesses	someone who is unhappy in his job
health services, flower design, or car repair	a type of school that provides career training

PARAGRAPH OUTLINE

Definition ....

1st Characteristic A. ....

    Detail   1. Because they offer short programs ....

    Detail   2. Not universities ....

2nd Characteristic B. ....

    Detail   1. ....

    Detail   2. Advantage for students who know what they want to do ....

3rd Characteristic C. Good for people interested in changing or finding new careers ....

    Detail   1. ....

    Detail   2. Someone who raised kids ....

4th Characteristic D. ....

    Detail   1. Can get work experience ....

    Detail   2. Can get job right away ....

B Definition in Academic Writing

Definition paragraphs are useful for **explaining words or ideas** that might be unknown or unfamiliar to a reader. This may be a word from another language, a technical term, or a concept. For example, a student writing about South Korean business culture may need to define the word *chaebol* (a multi-company business). Or a culinary student may want to explain what *julienning* is (cutting something into long strips).

In a definition paragraph, the **topic sentence** provides a brief definition. Like other types of paragraphs, the remaining sentences provide additional information through examples, explanations, descriptions, and other details. Unlike other types of paragraphs, however, the **concluding sentence** in a definition paragraph usually does not restate the topic sentence or main points. Instead, it may make a final comment on what is being described, for example, by saying why it's important or beneficial.

Read the two paragraphs. Which paragraph do you think better defines a *letter of recommendation*?

Paragraph 1

A Letter of Recommendation

A letter of recommendation is a letter that describes a student's character. It can help a student get accepted to a university because it shows that the student will be successful. The person who writes the letter knows the student very well, such as a high school teacher, school counselor, or member of the community. The letter includes information that describes the student's accomplishments and personal strengths. For example, the letter can tell a story about how a student overcame a challenge. The letter lets university staff see what kind of person the applicant is and helps them decide whether to admit the student. Students need to think carefully about who to ask to write this letter.

Paragraph 2

A Letter of Recommendation

When students apply to a university, they often need to include several letters of recommendation with the application. The people who write the letters of recommendation should know the student very well. I don't remember who I asked to write my letters of recommendation. The letters allow the university to see what kind of person the applicant is. Letters of recommendation, along with grades, exam results, and an interview, are used when considering whether or not to admit the student. They are therefore very important, and students need to think carefully about who to ask to write these letters.

It is clear that paragraph 1 is easier to understand. Why? The topic sentence defines what a letter of recommendation is, and the supporting sentences include detailed explanations and examples. Paragraph 2 has no topic sentence and is lacking in detail. In addition, it includes information that is not useful in helping the reader understand what a letter of recommendation is.

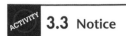 **3.3** Notice

Which of the beginning sentences in paragraph 1 or 2 defines a concept? What pronoun follows the category of "letter"?

WRITING TOPIC SENTENCES IN DEFINITION PARAGRAPHS

The topic sentence in a definition paragraph **introduces the word or idea** (what is being defined) and provides a **brief definition**. Don't try to include too much information in the topic sentence. You can use the rest of the paragraph to develop the ideas further.

Look at the topic sentence from paragraph 1 on page 139. Notice that it includes a topic, a category, and an identifier.

    TOPIC   CATEGORY   IDENTIFIER
A letter of recommendation is *a letter* that *describes a student's character.*

A **topic** is the idea you are defining. A **category** describes the general type or kind of idea it is. An **identifier** explains how it is different from other ideas in the same category. Look at some other examples below:

    TOPIC   CATEGORY   IDENTIFIER
A professor is *a teacher* who *teaches in a college or university.*

            TOPIC   CATEGORY   IDENTIFIER
I think that *patience* is *a virtue* that *is the most important for a parent.*

TOPIC SENTENCE WITH A DICTIONARY DEFINITION

Not every topic sentence will follow the pattern above. A topic sentence can also include a **dictionary definition** and sometimes the name of the dictionary you are using. Use verbs like *means, defines,* and *is defined as,* to give a definition. The topic sentence may also include a category and identifier.

*According to Cambridge Dictionaries Online, integrity **means** "honesty and the ability to know and do what is right."*

*The dictionary **defines** a test as questions about a topic. The questions assess a student's current ability.*

*An achievement test **is defined as** a test that is designed to measure how much a student has learned.*

3.4 Identify Features

Look at these four topic sentences. Circle the topic, underline the category, and double-underline the identifier.

1 Tutors are private teachers who often teach students one on one.

2 A transcript is an official document that lists all your classes and grades.

3 A thesaurus is a reference book that has words with the same meaning grouped together.

4 The dictionary defines a teaching assistant as a person who assists a professor with his or her class.

 3.5 Write Definitions

Write a topic sentence that defines each term. Use a dictionary to help.

1 The dictionary defines a high school principal as ....

....

2 According to my dictionary, graduation means ....

....

3 A diploma is defined as ....

....

4 The dictionary defines kindergarten as ....

....

3.6 Write Definitions

Complete these topic sentences with your own ideas. Add categories and identifiers.

1 A mid-term exam is ....

....

2 Clubs are ....

....

3 A lecturer is ....

....

4 An A+ is ....

....

3.7 Apply It to Your Writing

Work with a partner. Write three different topic sentence for your writing prompt on page 131. Decide which one you think is the best sentence. You may want to use these ideas later.

....

....

WAYS TO DEFINE WORDS IN A DEFINITION PARAGRAPH

There are several ways that supporting sentences and details describe a word so that the reader can really understand its characteristics. Often a writer has a unique – or special – perspective on the word that he or she wants to share. Below are some common ways to define a word:

1 Give **an example**.

   Tutors are private teachers who often teach students one on one. My brother is a math tutor for our neighbors' two kids, but sometimes I think he's also the babysitter.

2 Give **an explanation**.

   A transcript is an official document that lists all your classes and grades. It's part of a student's permanent academic record where everything is listed in one place.

3 **Compare** the concept to something that is similar and familiar to your readers.

   A thesaurus is a book that has words with the same meaning grouped together. It is similar to a dictionary, but it has synonyms and antonyms instead.

4 Say what the **word is not**.

   The dictionary defines a teaching assistant as a person who assists a professor with his or her class. A teaching assistant is not the actual professor, but sometimes I feel I learn more from the assistant!

3.8 Identify Supporting Sentences and Details

Read the definition paragraph. Then identify the type of each of the supporting sentences underlined below.

Elective Classes

An elective is a type of class that a student chooses to take. <u>It is not a class that is required</u> <u>for a student's major.</u> ⁽¹⁾ <u>A business student, for example, may take an elective class in music</u> <u>appreciation.</u> ⁽²⁾ An engineering student might take an elective in modern Chinese films. <u>Electives are similar to extracurricular activities because students choose what interests them.</u> ⁽³⁾ However, students do not receive a grade with an extracurricular activity. <u>Students do receive a</u> <u>grade when they take an elective.</u> ⁽⁴⁾ These appear on a transcript like any other class. Electives help give a student a balanced education.

1 Sentence 1 ....
  a gives an explanation   b says what the concept is not
2 Sentence 2 ....
  a gives an example   b compares the concept to something familiar
3 Sentence 3 ....
  a gives an explanation   b compares the concept to something familiar
4 Sentence 4 ....
  a gives an explanation   b gives an example

 3.9 Identify Supporting Sentences

Complete the definition paragraph using the phrases (a–e) below. Write the letters.

a A scholarship is not a loan.

b It is given to students who have excellent grades, do well in extracurricular activities, or have financial need.

c Some can also be used for housing, food, and other personal expenses.

d It is similar to a grant because the student does not have to pay the scholarship money back.

e A scholarship can be used for expenses that are directly related to a student's academic study, such as tuition, fees, and textbooks.

Scholarships

A scholarship is an award of money that helps a student further his or her education. .... ⁽¹⁾ (explanation). .... ⁽²⁾ (comparison). .... ⁽³⁾ (says what concept is not). .... ⁽⁴⁾ (example). However, there are many types of scholarships. .... ⁽⁵⁾ (explanation). A scholarship is very beneficial to a student's educational success.

3.10 Write Supporting Sentences

Work with a partner. Read the topic sentence below. Then write supporting sentences for each.

Topic sentence: A group project is a task that requires students to work together.

1 Explain the value of a group project.

....

....

2 Give an example of a group project you were a part of.

....

....

3 Say what a group project is similar to.

....

....

4 Say what a group project is not.

....

....

 3.11 Practice Writing

A Work with a partner. Use your sentences from Activity 3.10 above and other ideas to complete the paragraph.

A Group Project

A group project is a task that requires students to work together. ....

....

....

....

....

....

It's clear that group projects are an important part of academic study.

B Exchange your work with another pair. Read their paragraphs. Are the ideas clear?

ACTIVITY

3.12 Analyze Your Writing

YOUR TURN

Look back at your brainstorm on page 131. Choose three ideas and write supporting sentences. Use a variety of ways to support your topic sentences, such as examples, explanations, comparing, and saying what something is not.

_____

_____

_____

_____

_____

_____

Ⓐ Writing Skill: Paragraph Unity

All of the sentences in the paragraph need to be about the main idea in the topic sentence. This is called **paragraph unity**. These supporting sentences work together to describe, clarify, and explain that main idea. If supporting sentences do not directly relate to the main idea, it confuses the reader.

As you write, ask yourself if each sentence supports your main idea. If it does not, it may be irrelevant. Irrelevant sentences are those that are not related to the topic and, therefore, are not part of a unified paragraph.

In this example paragraph, an irrelevant sentence is crossed out. The opinion about the unfairness of the grading system is out of place in the middle of the explanation.

A Dean's List

A dean's list consists of students in higher education who get excellent grades during a semester in college or university. It is similar to an honor roll, but an honor roll is generally only used in high schools. To be on the dean's list, students usually need a G.P.A. of 3.5 or above. This means their grade point average for all classes must be above 3.5. ~~I think this is unfair and students who get 3.0 and above should be included~~. The G.P.A. is based on the A–F grading scale. For example, on this scale an A is 4, a B is 3, a C is 2, a D is 1, and an F is 0. It is an honor to be on the dean's list, and many students work hard to achieve this each semester.

 4.1 Analyze Irrelevant Sentences

Read the paragraph. Cross out the irrelevant sentence.

Homework

Homework is work that a teacher gives students to do at home. Homework can be an important part of a student's education. Besides learning from doing the homework, students also learn other important skills, such as responsibility and time management. It is very common for teachers to give homework in elementary, middle, and high school. Some teachers say they don't like to correct homework. In universities, homework becomes less common. The teacher may still assign work to do at home, but it's usually an "assignment," not homework. A teacher in a university is also less likely to check to see if a student has completed the work at home. It is the student's responsibility to make sure they have completed any work that is assigned by a teacher.

B Grammar for Writing: Subject Relative Clauses

A **subject relative clause** combines two ideas. We use subject clauses to **define, describe**, and to **give additional information** about someone or something without starting a new sentence. This makes your writing sound more natural because you don't have to repeat certain words. For example:

A transcript is an official document. A transcript lists all your classes and grades.

RELATIVE CLAUSE
A transcript is an official document <u>that lists all your classes and grades</u>.

SUBJECT RELATIVE CLAUSES	
1 A relative pronoun is the subject of a subject relative clause.	RELATIVE PRONOUN *A teaching assistant is a person **who** helps a professor with his or her class. (who = person)* RELATIVE PRONOUN *A dictionary is a book **that** provides definitions of words. (that = book)*
2 Use the relative pronoun *who* when it refers to a person. Avoid using *that* in academic writing.	*A teaching assistant is a person **who** helps a professor with his or her class.*
3 Use the relative pronoun *which* or *that* when it refers to a thing.	*A dictionary is a book **which/that** provides definitions of words.*
4 The verb in the relative clause agrees with the noun that the clause refers to.	*A tutor is a private <u>teacher</u> **who** often <u>teaches</u> students one on one.* *Letters of recommendation are <u>letters</u> **which/that** <u>help</u> a student get accepted to university.*

 4.2 Completion

Circle the correct relative pronoun.

1 Harvard is a university **who / which** is often ranked number 1 in the U.S.A.

2 In a dormitory, resident assistants are the people **who / which** are in charge of each floor.

3 A dictionary and thesaurus are two books **who / which** should be on every student's desk.

4 A college roommate is someone **who / which** often becomes a close friend.

5 A study buddy is someone **who / which** can help motivate you when necessary.

6 Texas and Florida are two states **who / which** are popular places for American students to vacation during spring break.

4.3 Sentence Combining

Join the sentences to make sentences with relative clauses.

1 Home schooling is a type of education. The education takes place at home rather than in a school.

....

....

....

2 Home schooling is an option. The option is becoming more and more popular.

....

....

....

3 A home-schooling parent is a type of teacher. A teacher is also a principal, a coach, a cook, and an administrator.

....

....

....

4 A home-schooler is a type of student. A student studies at home instead of at school.

....

....

....

5 State schools are places of learning. These places usually have affordable tuition.

....

....

....

Avoiding Common Mistakes

Research tells us that these are the most common mistakes that students make when using subject relative clauses in academic writing.

---

1 Use *who* for people and *that* for things. Do not use *that* for people and *who* for things.

                                    who
   An academic counselor is a person ~~that~~ helps students plan their courses.

                                  that
   A scholarship is an award of money ~~who~~ helps a student further his or her education.

2 The verb after a relative pronoun agrees with the noun that the pronoun modifies.

                                  want
   *This is extremely beneficial for **students** who ~~wants~~ to get a job right away.*

3 Do not use a subject pronoun after a relative pronoun.

   A diagnostic test is a test that ~~it~~ assesses a student's current ability.

4 Do not omit a subject relative pronoun.

                              who
   This is an advantage for those students ⌃ already know what they want to do.

 4.4 Editing Task

Find and correct four more mistakes in the paragraph below.

A Major

                              which
   In North America, a major is a specific subject ~~who~~ a student studies while working toward a college degree. Typically between a third and a half of a student's courses are part of his or her major. The other courses are known as core courses. These consist of classes that all students they have to take. Students usually need to choose a major by the end of their second year of study. Students who wants to can also choose two majors. This is called a double major. This is an advantage for students can't decide between two majors. Another option is choosing a major and a minor. A minor is similar to a major. It's also a specific subject area who a student studies, but students need to take fewer classes to achieve a minor. Choosing a major is clearly an important part of the college experience.

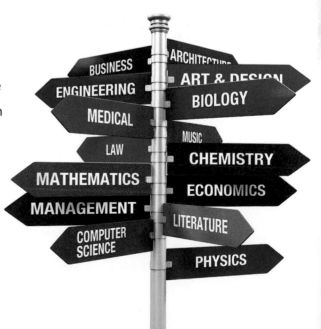

D Avoiding Plagiarism

Writers often use other writer's words to support their own ideas. When they do this, they make sure to give credit to the original author.

I understand that I can't copy and paste text into my work because it is plagiarizing. I also heard that when I start to write essays and do research, I can use the exact words of another writer to help me support my ideas. How do writers avoid plagiarism when they want to use other people's ideas?
– Irina

Dear Irina,

Sometimes when you do research, you might find a perfect sentence from another writer. When that happens, you can use those words if you put the <u>exact</u> words in quotation marks. You must also say where you found the original information by citing your source. Be careful not to do this too often. You want most of your essay to be in your own words.

Sincerely,

Professor Wright

QUOTING OTHERS

There are two things to think about when you use quotes: what to quote and how to quote.

WHAT TO QUOTE	EXAMPLE
1 Choose quotes carefully. There should not be too many quotes in your paragraph or essay. 2 Use quotes that support your main idea. 3 Quote words, phrases, or sentences that • use unique wording or unforgettable language; • say something strong, dramatic, or moving; • include something that is memorable or historically significant; • give an idea that is written very clearly or hard to paraphrase.	Original graduation speech by Ariana Huffington including a unique, strong, memorable idea: *Wherever we look around the world, we see very smart leaders – in politics, in business, in media – making terrible decisions. **What they're lacking is not IQ, but wisdom.** Which is no surprise, since it's never been harder to tap into our own wisdom.*

HOW TO QUOTE	EXAMPLE
1 Write the author's name, if known, in the same sentence as the quote. 2 Include information about the author's background, if it is known. 3 Put the exact words in quotation marks (" ").	*In her 2013 speech at Smith College,* **Ariana Huffington, an author and journalist,** *says that world leaders are smart, but their decisions are poor. She explains that* **"what they're lacking is not IQ, but wisdom."**

 4.5 Practice

Read the original text. Then read the student paragraph and underline words that need quotation marks.

Original text by Lizzie Wann, Content Director for Bridgeport Education

Finally, one of the greatest benefits to having a college education is passing on the legacy to your children. Children of a college grad are more likely to have a better quality of life and pursue extended education themselves. Those children also have a much easier time getting into good schools because their parents have emphasized the importance of an education to them.

Student paragraph

College education has many advantages. According to Lizzie Wann, Content Director for Bridgeport Education, one of the most important advantages is passing on the legacy. She says that if a person graduates from college, that person's children will probably enjoy a better quality of life and pursue extended education themselves. Also, it will be easier for them to get into better schools if their mother or father has made it clear how important it is to get an education.

In this section, you will follow the writing process to complete the final draft of your paragraph.

STEP 1: BRAINSTORM

Work with a partner. Follow the steps below to brainstorm more ideas for your topic.

1   First, read the student's brainstorm. She wrote many ideas from the cluster diagram she used to reflect on her topic in Section 1, on page 130. Finally, she deleted the ideas that she thought would not work in her paragraph.

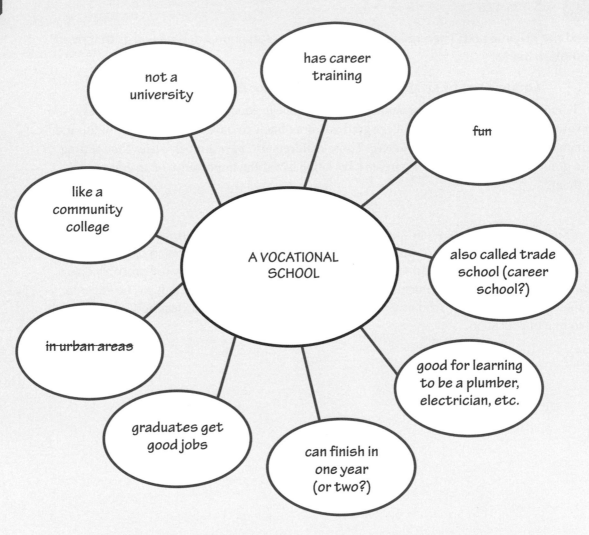

2   Now read your writing prompt again. Then review the ideas that you brainstormed in Section 1, page 131. Write the best ones in the cluster diagram on page 153. Add ideas from the Your Turns that you completed in the unit. Finally, brainstorm more ideas. You will probably not use every idea, but it is good to write as many ideas as possible.

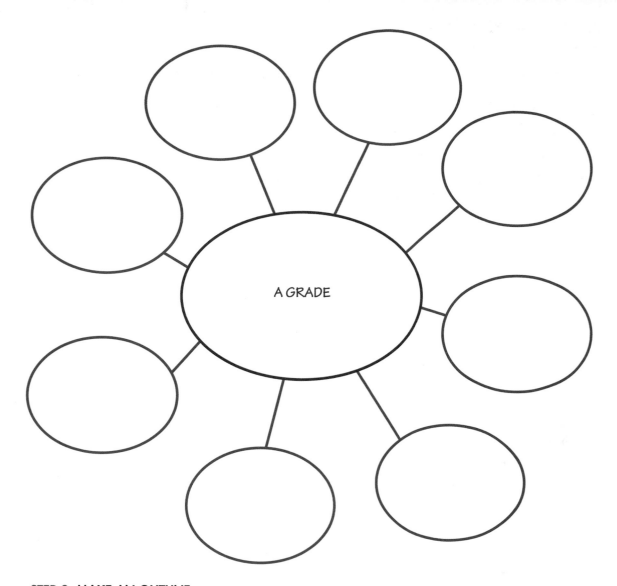

A GRADE

STEP 2: MAKE AN OUTLINE

Complete the outline below with ideas for your paragraph from Step 1.

PARAGRAPH OUTLINE

Definition	....
1st Characteristic	A. ....
Detail	1. ....
Detail	2. ....

(CONTINUED)

2nd Characteristic	B.	_____
Detail	1.	_____
Detail	2.	_____
3rd Characteristic	C.	_____
Detail	1.	_____
Detail	2.	_____
4th Characteristic	D.	_____
Detail	1.	_____
Detail	2.	_____

STEP 3: WRITE YOUR FIRST DRAFT

Now it's time to write your first draft. Here are some suggestions on how to get started.

1 Use your outline and the sentences you wrote in the Your Turns and in Step 2 above.

2 Focus on making your ideas as clear as possible.

3 Add a title.

After you finish, read your paragraph and check for basic errors.

1 Check that all sentences have subjects and verbs.

2 Go through and look at every comma. Is it correct? Should it be a period?

3 Check that you have used a comma after adverb clauses when they start a sentence.

4 Make sure your topic sentence and supporting sentences are clear.

STEP 4: WRITE YOUR FINAL DRAFT

1 After you receive feedback on your first draft, review it carefully. Fix any errors.

2 Make a note of errors that were most frequent (misspellings, using commas instead of periods, missing verbs). Try to avoid them as you write.

3 Review the Academic Vocabulary and Academic Collocations from this unit. Are there any that you can add to your paragraph?

4 Turn to page 241 and use the Self-Editing Review to check your work one more time.

5 Write your final draft and hand it in.

6 DESCRIPTIVE PARAGRAPHS
CULTURAL STUDIES: CULTURAL LANDMARKS

"We shape our buildings; thereafter they shape us."

Winston Churchill
(1874–1965)

About the Author:

Winston Churchill was a British politician and prime minister during the 1940s and 1950s.

Work with a partner. Read the quotation about buildings. Then answer the questions.

1 The author is saying that some buildings, such as places of worship or museums, influence our feelings and behavior. Do you agree that buildings can shape, or influence, people? How?

2 Describe your favorite building.

3 How does the building you described above influence you?

Ⓐ Connect to Academic Writing

In this unit, you will learn skills to help you explain how an object looks in a descriptive paragraph. You already know many of the skills to describe things because you do it in your everyday life. For example, you might tell a friend about an amazing building that you saw on vacation or explain a club or restaurant so well that you persuade your friend to go with you.

Ⓑ Reflect on the Topic

In this section, you will look at a writing prompt and reflect on it. Throughout the unit, you will develop ideas about this prompt. You will use these ideas to practice skills that are necessary to write your paragraph.

The writing prompt below was used for the Student Model paragraph on page 162. The student reflected on his topic and used a cluster diagram to brainstorm his ideas. This helped him think about all the details he might include in his paragraph.

WRITING PROMPT: Describe an object that is important to a culture you know. Explain any symbolism in the object.

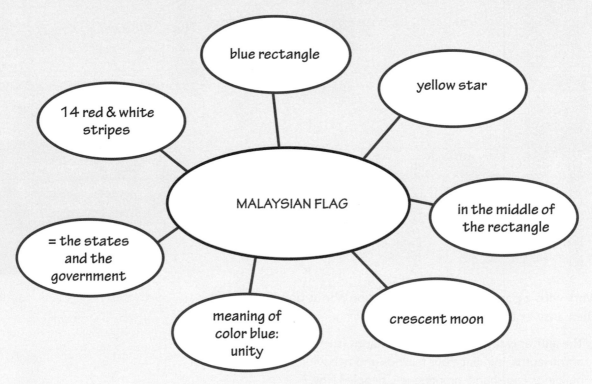

 1.1 Notice

Work with a partner. Describe the characteristics of a flag you know well.

Read the prompt and follow the directions below.

WRITING PROMPT: Describe a place or landmark of national importance in a country you know. Explain why it is important.

1   Think of a city or country you know well. Think about places or landmarks that are important there.

2   Choose one place from your list and create a cluster diagram for it. First, write your topic in the circle in the middle.

3   Then think about everything you know about this place or object. Put this information in the other circles. Add or delete circles if necessary.

4   Compare cluster diagrams with a partner.

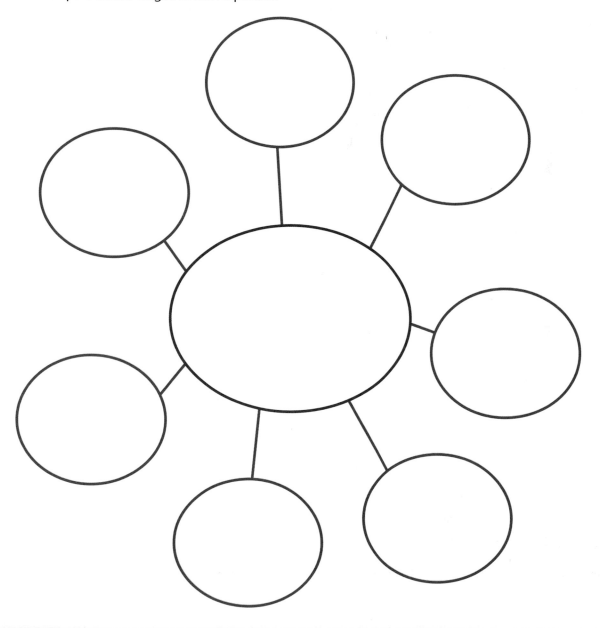

In this section, you will learn academic language that you can use in your descriptive paragraph. You will also notice how a professional writer uses this language.

Ⓐ Academic Vocabulary

The words below appear throughout the unit. They are from the Academic Word List or the General Service List. Using these words in your writing will make your ideas clearer and your writing more academic.

area (n)	cost (n)	design (v)	represent (v)
century (n)	cultural (adj)	religious (adj)	symbol (n)

 2.1 Focus on Meaning

Work with a partner. Read the sentences. Decide the meaning of the words in bold and circle the correct definitions.

1 Five different colored rings are the **symbol** of the Olympic Games. **Symbol** means

   a a sign of something else.   b a decoration on your fingers.

2 The Malaysian flag was designed over half a **century** ago, in 1947. **Century** means

   a a long time.   b a period of 100 years.

3 The large **area** in the left of the painting is filled with pale blue sky. **Area** means

   a a color.   b a part of a place.

4 The green color in the Brazilian flag **represents** the old royal family of the House of Braganza. **Represent** means

   a to fly over something.   b to be a sign of; symbolize.

5 Architects **designed** a giant glass window at the front of the building. **Design** means

   a to look at something such as a house in different types of light.   b to make or draw plans for something.

6 Residents want to build a new museum, but the **cost** will be very high. The city can't afford it. **Cost** means

   a a strong interest in something.   b an amount of money needed to buy or do something.

7 In his country, there is a **cultural** belief in the importance of success. **Cultural** means:

   a relating to the system of belief in a god or gods.   b relating to the habits and traditions of a society.

8 Some landmarks are **religious**. For example, some are important to people of the Christian faith. **Religious** means

   a relating to the system of belief in a god or gods.   b relating to ideas about statues.

B Academic Phrases

Research tells us that the phrases in bold below are commonly used in academic writing.

ACTIVITY 2.2 Focus on Purpose

Work with a partner. Read the paragraph. Then match the phrases in bold to the purpose, or reason why, the writer used them. Write the letters.

A Beloved Statue in Rio de Janeiro

The statue Christo Redemptor in Rio de Janeiro is loved for its beauty. **A good example of** its beauty is the face. The expression is calm and gentle. It makes me feel calm, too. **Another example is** the position of the figure. He stands with open arms. It looks like he is embracing the whole city. It is a powerful symbol of love. The huge statue stands on top of Corcovado Mountain. **In addition to** its beauty, the statue is in an impressive place. There is an amazing view from Corcovado. Visitors can see the whole city, beaches, and gardens. For many people Christo Redemptor represents the beauty of the city it overlooks.

PHRASE	PURPOSE
.... 1 In addition to ... ,	a introduce the first example
.... 2 A good example [of ....] is ...	b introduce another example
.... 3 Another example [of ....] is ...	c add an idea

C Writing in the Real World

You will read an article titled "Three Famous Landmarks." The author of the article uses descriptive writing to create pictures that make her ideas clearer.

Before you read, answer these questions: Which landmarks and monuments does the writer think are the most famous? What is important about each one?

Now read the article. Think about your answer to the questions as you read.

THREE FAMOUS LANDMARKS

by Jeanne Fedowski

Many landmarks tell a story about a country, an ancient culture, or a religious belief. Some also tell of simple human emotions – hope, curiosity, and love.

Great Pyramid of Khufu, Egypt

1   A group of huge monuments rises above Giza, Egypt. Today, we think of these monuments as a **symbol** of Egypt. However, these structures are so ancient that even people two thousand years ago did not remember their builders or purpose. Probably the most famous of these monuments is the Great Pyramid of Khufu. Almost five thousand years ago, the people of Egypt built it. It was a tomb[1] for their pharaoh, or king. In their religion, they believed that the pharaoh was a connection between them and the gods. Their priority was to keep the pharaoh safe, in life and in death. To ancient Egyptians, the pyramids also **represented** hope. The people hoped that the deceased king became a god. Then he could keep harmony[2] in the world.

[1]**tomb**: a building or place underground for a dead person
[2]**harmony**: a pleasing combination of different parts

Stonehenge, England

2   At about the same time as the Egyptians built the pyramids, the people of ancient England built Stonehenge. Stonehenge is a circle of huge standing stones. The largest weighs over 50 tons (about 100,000 pounds). Inside this stone circle, there is another ring of stones. Nobody knows for certain about the **religious** beliefs of the Stonehenge builders. We know, though, that the builders **designed** the stone circle carefully to allow people to study the sky. Perhaps they did this to predict[3] changes in seasons. In addition, archaeologists believe that Stonehenge was a place for religious ceremonies. They believe these ceremonies let people remember their ancestors.[4]

[3]**predict**: to say that an event or action will happen in the future
[4]**ancestor**: any member of your family from long ago, for example the grandparents of your grandparents

Taj Mahal, India

3 Today, the Taj Mahal is a symbol of India, but it also symbolizes love. In the seventeenth **century**, Shah Jahan built the beautiful buildings and gardens, at great **cost**, as a tomb for his deceased wife. At the center is the brilliant white dome, which rises high above the **area**. At the top of this dome is a lotus flower, another symbol of India, and around this large dome are four smaller ones. Exquisite[5] decoration and Islamic writing cover the buildings.

4 **Cultural** landmarks are the heart and soul of any place. But some seem important to *all* of us – not just to the people who live in that place.

[5]**exquisite**: especially beautiful

 2.3 Check Your Understanding

Answer the questions.

1 How are the Great Pyramid of Khufu and the Taj Mahal similar?

2 What do we *know* about Stonehenge? What do some people *believe* about Stonehenge?

3 What other cultural landmarks do you know? Who built them and why?

 2.4 Notice the Features of Descriptive Writing

Answer the questions.

1 Read the paragraph about the Taj Mahal again. Underline all parts of the Taj Mahal that the writer describes. Which part do you think is the most important to the writer? Why do you think so?

2 Circle words and phrases that tell you where these parts are.

In Section 1, you saw how the writer of the Student Model reflected on his topic. In this section, you will analyze the final draft of his paragraph. You will learn how to develop ideas for your own paragraph.

Ⓐ Student Model

Read the prompt and answer the questions.

WRITING PROMPT: Describe an object that is important to a culture you know. Explain any symbolism in the object.

1 Read the title of the Student Model. What is a "cultural landmark"?

2 Look at the photo of the Malaysian flag. What do you think it symbolizes about the country?

Read the paragraph twice. The first time, think about your answers to the questions above. The second time, answer the questions in the Analyze Writing Skills boxes. This will help you notice key features of a descriptive paragraph.

STUDENT MODEL

A Flag as a Cultural Landmark

The flag of Malaysia is a famous **symbol** of my country. It is beautiful and colorful. The flag is red, white, blue, and yellow. It tells important information about our great country. The big part of the flag has fourteen red and white stripes. The stripes **represent** the states and the government. At the top and on the left there is a blue rectangle. The color blue symbolizes unity. People of Malaysia are from different cultures, and they have different religions. However, we try to work together. I am proud of my people for this! In the middle of the blue **area** is a big yellow star and a crescent moon. Yellow is the color of the king and queen. The moon is a **religious** symbol. It symbolizes Islam, which is the main religion of Malaysia. Our flag is also called Jalur Gemilang. It means "Stripes of Glory." I love my flag because I love my country.

1 Analyze Writing Skills

Circle three adjectives that describe the flag in the opening two sentences.

2 Analyze Writing Skills

Underline two phrases that tell where the blue rectangle is.

3 Analyze Writing Skills

Underline the phrase that tells where on the flag to find the star and crescent moon.

4 Analyze Writing Skills

What words describe the star? Circle them.

3.1 Check Your Understanding

Answer the questions.

1 How many stripes are on the flag of Malaysia? What do they represent?

2 What example of "unity" does the student writer give? How does he feel about his people?

3 What can you see in the middle of the dark blue area? What do these two things represent?

 3.2 Outline the Writer's Ideas

Complete this outline for "A Flag as a Cultural Landmark." Use the phrases in the box.

represent the states and the government	yellow = color of the king and queen
beautiful and colorful	different people try to work together
blue rectangle	

PARAGRAPH OUTLINE

Topic Sentence	The flag of Malaysia is a famous symbol of my country.
Supporting Idea	A.
Detail	1. Red, white, blue, and yellow
Supporting Idea	B. Fourteen red and white stripes
Detail	1.
Supporting Idea	C.
Detail	1. Color symbolizes unity
Detail	2.
Supporting Idea	D. Yellow star and crescent moon
Detail	1.
Detail	2. Moon = a religious symbol (= Islam)
Concluding Sentence	I love my flag because I love my country.

B Descriptive Paragraphs

A good descriptive paragraph lets readers experience the object or place in the same way as the writer does. Readers can see and experience it clearly in their minds. As a result, they can understand the writer's feelings and purpose for writing about it.

In academic writing, writers use description for different purposes. For example, they might describe a historical object so that the readers can understand its beauty, symbolism, and importance to a culture.

In general, all descriptive paragraphs have the same parts as most paragraphs:

- a topic sentence that tells the reader what the writer will write about
- supporting sentences and details that give information about the topic sentence
- a concluding sentence that often restates the topic sentence

However, in a descriptive paragraph, writers have a variety of ways to describe an object and talk about its significance. Below is an explanation of how the parts of a descriptive paragraph are different from other paragraphs.

TOPIC SENTENCES

The **topic sentence** in a descriptive paragraph introduces the person, place, or thing that the writer will describe. In this topic sentence, the **controlling idea** tells the writer's focus for the paragraph. The focus is what will get the most attention. The example below shows that the focus is on the symbolism of the flag:

TOPIC   CONTROLLING IDEA

The flag of Malaysia is the most famous symbol of my country.

In a descriptive paragraph, the focus in the controlling idea is sometimes as simple as a single adjective. The example below shows the focus is on the beauty of the building:

TOPIC   CONTROLLING IDEA

The Taj Mahal is one of the most beautiful buildings in the world.

As in other paragraphs, the topic sentence of a descriptive paragraph must answer the prompt. This is helpful to you, the writer, because the prompt usually suggests what the focus should be. One way to make sure you have a clear focus is to include an important word or phrase from the prompt in the topic sentence.

WRITING PROMPT: What is one important cultural landmark in your hometown? Describe it.

An important cultural landmark in New York City is Central Park.

 3.3 Notice

Read these prompts and topic sentences. Circle the words and phrases in each topic sentence that come from the prompt.

1 **WRITING PROMPT:** If visitors to your city want to see a landmark of religious importance, where should these people go? Describe this landmark.

Visitors to Moscow should go to St. Basil Cathedral if they want to see a religious landmark.

2 **WRITING PROMPT:** A tourist from another country has only one day to spend in your hometown. Which landmark should this person visit? Why? Describe it.

A tourist in Athens should spend the day at the Acropolis because it is the symbol of ancient Greece.

3 **WRITING PROMPT:** What is a famous piece of art that you do not like? Why? Describe it.

Although it is very famous, I do not like Da Vinci's Mona Lisa *because this woman's face is not attractive.*

4 **WRITING PROMPT:** What is one landmark that people probably think of when they think about your country? Do you think it represents your culture? Why or why not?

When people think about Brazil, the statue Christo Redemptor is probably the cultural landmark that they think of.

 3.4 Choose Topic Sentences

Choose the best topic sentence for each paragraph. Write the letter.

1

.... The problem began during the building process in the 12th century. The tower did not stand straight. Today, it still leans at 3.97°. However, it is a beautiful building. It consists of eight stories that look like a tall, round, white cake. Inside, there are 294 steps. At the top, there are seven bells. It is a bell tower, but that was not its main purpose. Its main purpose was to attract people to the cathedral that is behind it. It always achieved this purpose. Today, tourists from all over the world come to see it. They are attracted to its lovely imperfection.

a For most people, the Tower of Pisa is amazing.

b In Italy there is a tower that looks like a white cake.

c The Tower of Pisa is famous for its imperfection.

2

.... *A souk* is a huge outdoor market. In a typical *souk*, there are big crowds of people. To their right and left, there are hundreds of shops. These shops are full of colorful things to buy. You can find almost anything in a *souk*. A good example is the area with shops that sell clothing or fabric. You can make your own clothing with this fabric. Another example is the section for shoes. Next to this, another area sells carpets for your floor or blankets for your bed. Then there are the wonderful food shops. They have mountains of nuts, spices, and fruits. The owner sits at the center of his or her shop. When you talk with this person, it is important to spend time discussing price. Often, you share a glass of mint tea with the shop owner. In this way, a visit to a *souk* is a true Moroccan experience.

a There are many *souks* in Morocco.

b A visitor to a *souk* gets a wonderful taste of Morocco.

c I visited a *souk* when I went to Morocco.

ACTIVITY **3.5** Apply It to Your Writing

Work with a partner. Write three different topic sentences for your writing prompt on page 157. Decide which one you think is the best sentence.

....

....

....

....

....

....

SUPPORTING SENTENCES AND DETAILS

In a descriptive paragraph, the **supporting sentences** and **details** make the "picture" clear in the mind of the reader. However, they do not only tell how the object looks. They also give information about the focus in the topic sentence. For example, they give an explanation of the object's symbolism, purpose, cultural or religious importance, or personal experiences with the object. Look at the example below:

Topic sentence:

The flag of Malaysia is the most famous <u>symbol</u> of my country.

Supporting sentence:

In the middle of the blue area is a big yellow star and a crescent moon.

Details about the supporting sentence:

Yellow is <u>the color of the king and queen</u>. The moon is a religious <u>symbol</u>. It <u>symbolizes Islam</u>, which is one of the main religions of Malaysia.

DESCRIBING LOCATION

In descriptive writing, it is often necessary to say where things are. To describe a photograph or painting, use the following **prepositions of place** and **prepositional phrases:**

in the middle / in the center/at the center	*on the left*
at the bottom	*in front (of)*
at the top / on top (of)	*in back (of) / behind*
on the right	*next to*

3.6 Write Supporting Details

Look at the painting *The Red Oldtimer*. Complete the paragraph with prepositions of place and prepositional phrases from the box.

behind	at the bottom	on the left	in the middle	next to	in front of

A Picture of the Past and Future

The painting of *The Red Oldtimer* represents the past and the future together. Most of this unusual painting seems to be from the past. _____ (1) of the picture, there is an old red car. _____ (2) of the car, there is an old building with open green shutters on the second floor. A cowboy is walking _____ (3) the car. On the right, a low wall is _____ (4) an old two-story building that has three balconies. _____ (5) of the painting, we see a drain for water in the old stone street. However, two details seem to be from the future. _____ (6) the old town, there is a huge spaceship in the sky over a very modern city. The painting makes us think. Maybe this strange place is the *present*, where past and future come together.

3.7 Apply It to Your Writing

Look at the ideas you wrote in Section 1 on page 157. Write sentences with prepositions of place and prepositional phrases about your place or object.

....

....

....

ORGANIZING IDEAS IN SPATIAL ORDER

It is important to organize your ideas clearly and logically in a descriptive paragraph. This helps a reader more easily understand your description. Writers often organize their ideas using **spatial order** – where things are located in space.

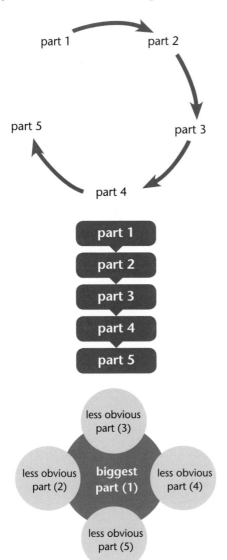

For example, one way to organize ideas is describing the parts **clockwise** – the direction of the hands of a clock. Begin with the top of the picture. Then describe something to the right of this, and so on.

At the top, and on the left, there is a dark blue area. In the middle of this area, there are two symbols of Malaysia, a big yellow star with fourteen points and a crescent moon. To the right of the dark blue area is the biggest part of the flag. This part has fourteen red and white stripes.

Another way to organize a paragraph is describing something from **top to bottom** or, the opposite, from **bottom to top**. For example:

The bottom of the Christo Redemptor statue stands on top of Corcovado Mountain. In the middle of the statue are his open arms. It looks like he is embracing the whole city. At the top of the statue, a calm, gentle expression is on his face.

Another way to organize ideas is by going from **biggest to smallest**. In other words, starting with the feature people usually notice first and then describing smaller or less noticeable parts.

The biggest part of the flag has fourteen red and white stripes. At the top, and on the left, there is also a smaller dark blue area. In the middle of this area, there are two symbols of Malaysia. On the left is a crescent moon. On the right is a yellow star with fourteen points.

ACTIVITY **3.8** Notice

Look at the paragraph for Activity 3.6 on page 167. Check (✓) the type of spatial order the writer used.

☐ clockwise

☐ top to bottom

☐ biggest to smallest

ACTIVITY **3.9** Order Supporting Sentences

Look at the painting and paragraph in Activity 3.6. Choose a different type of spatial order and rewrite the paragraph on a separate piece of paper.

ACTIVITY **3.10** Apply It to Your Writing

Go to the ideas you wrote in Section 1 on page 157. Write which way you might organize your ideas spatially. Write why you think this is the best way to organize your ideas.

....

....

....

....

ADDING DETAILS TO A DESCRIPTIVE PARAGRAPH

In a descriptive paragraph, each supporting sentence describes one part of the object. After each supporting sentence, there is usually at least one **detail** about it. Sometimes these details give more description. Sometimes they give more information. This information can be symbolism, meaning, purpose, cultural or religious importance, or how something works.

Look at the photo of the Oval Office below. Match each detail (a–f) to its supporting sentence.

Supporting Sentences

1 Behind the desk, there are two flags.

   Detail: ....   Detail: ....

2 There are three tall windows at the back of the office.

   Detail: ....

3 At the center of the carpet is the presidential seal.

   Detail: ....

4 The president's desk is in front of the windows.

   Detail: ....

5 On the walls, there are famous paintings from American history.

   Detail: ....

Details

a These windows let in light from the Rose Garden.

b Each president chooses paintings that he likes.

c The flag on the left is the U.S. flag.

d The flag on the right is the president's flag.

e It is a large desk with exquisite decoration; it symbolizes the president's power.

f There are many symbols of the United States on this seal.

3.12 Write Supporting Sentences and Details

Use the sentences from Activity 3.11 to complete the paragraph below on a separate piece of paper. Choose a spatial order.

The Oval Office

The Oval Office, in Washington, D.C., symbolizes the American presidency. ....

....

3.13 Practice Your Writing

Go to the ideas you wrote in Section 1 on page 157. Note down some details which you could use in your final draft.

....

....

....

CONCLUDING SENTENCES

In a descriptive paragraph, the concluding sentence usually includes a word or phrase from the controlling idea. This reminds the reader of the focus and makes the paragraph seem complete.

3.14 Choose a Concluding Sentence

Choose the best concluding sentence for the descriptive paragraph in Activity 3.11.

a Clearly, the Oval Office, in the White House, is very beautiful.

b In conclusion, the Oval Office is an expression of each president.

c In short, the Oval Office symbolizes both the president and his job.

3.15 Apply It to Your Writing

Work with a partner. Write three different concluding sentences for your writing prompt on page 157. Decide which one you think is the best sentence.

....

....

....

....

....

In this section, you will learn the writing and grammar skills that will help make your writing more sophisticated and accurate.

Ⓐ Writing Skill: Adding Details with Adjectives and Adverbs

Writers use **adjectives** and **adverbs** in their descriptions to create a clear and interesting picture in their reader's mind. Below are some rules for using adjectives and adverbs.

USING ADJECTIVES

1 An adjective usually comes before the noun or after a linking verb (*be, become, seem,* or *look*).	ADJECTIVE NOUN *Stonehenge is an **ancient** structure.* SUBJECT ADJECTIVE *A flag is **portable**, so we can carry it.*
2 Adjectives give more detail to nouns in a sentence.	*Stonehenge is a circle of **huge** stones.* *At the center is the **brilliant white** dome.*

USING ADVERBS

Most adverbs end in *-ly*. They usually come after the verb (or after the verb + object). Sometimes they come before the verb.	VERB ADVERB *The man waves **proudly** as he rides his horse.* ADVERB VERB *The man **proudly** waves as he rides his horse.*
Good writers don't use *too* many adverbs.	*The man waves proudly, ~~excitedly, and enthusiastically~~, as he rides his horse*

  4.1 Analyze Descriptive Language

Circle the adjectives. Underline the nouns that they describe. Double-underline the linking verbs.

1 A famous symbol of Japan is the Great Buddha of Kamakura. This beautiful statue is huge – 13.35 meters high. His relaxed hands are in his lap, in the lotus position. Around his face, his hair is in tight curls. His face looks peaceful. This statue has religious importance in Japan.

2 An incredible landmark in Moscow is St. Basil's Cathedral, from the 16ᵗʰ century. The cathedral is a colorful collection of churches. A visitor will notice the bright red, green, blue, yellow, and gold colors. It also has an interesting characteristic. Its beautiful domes look like fire going up to the sky.

Great Buddah of Kamakura, Japan

4.2 Notice

Circles the adverbs and underline the verbs they describe.

A Picture of a Place and Time

A painting by Renoir (perfectly) represents comfort in 19th century France. In *Luncheon of the Boating Party*, men and women relax lazily after lunch on a hot summer day. A table is covered with a white tablecloth. On this table, there are empty glasses and plates, some bottles, and fruit. Some people sit sleepily around the table. Others stand and talk quietly with each other. One woman plays with a cute little dog. It sits happily on the table in front of her. I think this painting is very interesting. It shows us something about everyday life over one hundred years ago. It shows us how comfortably some people lived.

4.3 Put It All Together

Complete this paragraph about the Statue of Liberty. Use adjectives and adverbs from the box. Two are extra.

ancient	completely	long	strong-looking
beautifully	huge	small	

A Statue in New York Harbor

The Statue of Liberty is a symbol of the United States. The landmark, also called "Lady Liberty," stands on an island in New York Harbor. This statue looks .... (1) from a distance. However, it looks very big when you are close. Lady Liberty is a .... (2) woman. In her right hand, she holds a torch high over her head. This torch symbolizes light. She is lighting the road to freedom for new immigrants. She wears a .... (3) robe, like the clothing on an .... (4) Greek statue. She also wears a crown on her head. The crown is a symbol of the continents. The statue looks green because it is made of copper. In time, copper .... (5) changes from golden brown to green. In addition to representing the United States, Lady Liberty is also a symbol of freedom.

4.4 Practice Your Writing

Look back at your ideas in Section 1 page 157. Write adjectives and adverbs that you think will make the description of your place or object clearer.

....

....

ⓑ Grammar for Writing: *There is* and *There are*

Writers often use **There is / There are** to point out the presence of an object or to state a fact.

THERE IS AND THERE ARE	
1 Use *there is* when the first noun in a list is singular.	*There is one large **dome** and several smaller ones.*
2 Use *there are* when the first noun is plural.	*There are several small **domes** and one large one.*
3 You can use *some* after *there are*.	*There are some exquisite decorations.*
4 For the negative, use *there is/are no*.	*There are no **pictures** of people in most Islamic art.*
5 Writers often follow *there is/are* sentences with *It/They* sentences to give more details about the nouns.	*There is a big yellow star. **It** represents the country.*
There is and There are with Prepositional Phrases	
1 Use *there is / are* with a noun and a prepositional phrase.	*There are two symbols **in the middle of the flag**.*
2 Add a comma after the prepositional phrase.	*Inside the stone circle, there is another ring of stones.*

 4.5 Write *There is* and *There are*

A Fill in the blanks with *there is* or *there are*.

A Famous Painting by Van Gogh

Van Gogh's *Café Terrace at Night* is a brilliant painting of a coffee house. This painting shows a scene at night, but most of it isn't dark. Instead, ... (1) yellows, greens, and blues. .... (2) three sources of light. On the left, ... (3) a lantern that shines on the terrace. .... (4) people sitting at the tables and people walking on the street in front of the café. At the top of the painting, ... (5) another source of light: a sky filled with stars. .... (6) a shop on the right. Light comes from its windows. The only dark area is in the background.

B In the paragraph above, find prepositional phrases of place and underline them.

Avoiding Common Mistakes

Research tells us that these are the most common mistakes that students make when using *There is* and *There are* in academic writing.

1 Use *there is* with singular or noncount nouns. Use *there are* with plural nouns.

       are
There ~~is~~ fourteen stripes on the flag.

       is
There ~~are~~ a big blue area in the corner.

2 Remember to use *there* – not *it* or *they* – when you explain what exists in a place, a piece of art, or an object.

          there
In the photo, ~~they~~ are trees next to the fountain.

3 In speaking, *there are* sounds like *they're*. Do not confuse them in writing.

  There are
~~They're~~ two symbols in the center of the flag.

 ACTIVITY **4.6** Editing Task

Find and correct four more mistakes in the paragraph below.

Mount Rushmore National Memorial

                there
In the state of South Dakota, ~~it~~ is a huge stone monument. It is at the top of a mountain in the beautiful Black Hills. On this mountain, they are the massive heads of U.S. presidents. They're four of them: George Washington, Thomas Jefferson, Theodore Roosevelt, and Abraham Lincoln. This monument is a popular place for people on vacation. There is almost three million people who visit the area each year. However, not everyone enjoys this monument. They're many Native Americans who are unhappy about it. For them, this land has cultural and religious importance.

C Avoiding Plagiarism

Writers often share ideas, but how do you know when sharing becomes too much?

My friends and I have a study group. We work on our assignments together and help each other brainstorm ideas. If I use an idea from a friend, is it plagiarism?
– Meifen

Dear Meifen,

Good question! Writers often get ideas from other writers. It's great to get an idea or two from a friend, but be careful that all of your ideas aren't from someone else. The most important thing to remember is that your instructor wants to read what you have to say, not what your friend or someone else has to say.

Sometimes writers even get ideas from their own writing. You must write something new for each assignment and not reuse previous assignments.

Best regards,

Professor Wright

SHARING IDEAS

Brainstorming with others is a great way to come up with ideas. Sometimes, reflecting on your own previous writing assignments helps, too. Follow the guidelines below to understand what is plagiarism and what is not plagiarism when sharing ideas.

Do

1 Always use your own ideas for writing assignments. Remember that your instructor wants to read your ideas, not the ideas of your friends.

2 If you get a good idea from a friend during brainstorms, good! That's what brainstorms are for, BUT write the idea in your own words and explain it in your own way.

Don't

1 Don't reuse your writing assignments from other classes. Changing words or a few sentences is NOT acceptable.

2 Don't copy and paste ideas from papers by other students or from the Internet. This is plagiarism.

Sometimes assignments in classes are similar, but do not reuse them. Choose a different way to write about the topic so that you are challenging yourself and improving your English. Discuss ideas with your instructor.

Read the examples below. Which contain plagiarism? Explain your answers to a partner.

1 Roberto talked to his friend about an assignment and wrote down everything his friend said. Roberto added a title and then submitted the paragraph.

2 Susie wrote a paragraph about the CN Tower last semester for a descriptive essay. She's going to use the same paragraph, but she's going to change the introductory sentence and the concluding sentence.

3 Carol found a great paragraph online. She hates writing and thinks that this paragraph says what she thinks perfectly. She copied the paragraph exactly.

4 Mei brainstormed some topics with her friends. She used one or two ideas from the group, and used them to come up with more of her own. She wrote a paragraph in her own words.

5 WRITE YOUR PARAGRAPH

In this section, you will follow the writing process to complete the final draft of your paragraph.

STEP 1: BRAINSTORM

In this unit, you will continue your brainstorm using a **freewrite**.

Work with a partner. Follow the steps below to brainstorm more ideas for your topic.

1 Read the freewrite that the writer of the Student Model on page 162 did for his topic. Notice how the writer wrote down everything he could think of in the freewrite, but he chose only the ideas that he felt were the most important.

> A flag / landmark. It has meaning it's the symbol of a country. We can find it in many public places such as schools, my neighbor has one in front of his house. example = the flag of Malaysia (my country). Colorful! there is several symbols. One is a crescent moon (symbolizes Islam, the religion of Malaysia). and they're fourteen red and white stripes. Another symbol = a big yellow star with fourteen points (means the country). crescent and star in a dark blue area, top of the flag (and on the left). Mohamed Hamzah, an architect, designed the flag in 1947. a flag is portable we can carry easily this symbol anywhere. I love my flag!

2 Now read your writing prompt again. Then review the ideas that you brainstormed in Section 1, page 157.

WRITING PROMPT: Describe a place or object of national importance in a country you know. Explain why it is important.

3 Now start your freewrite. As you freewrite, do not worry about paragraph structure or grammar. It is important to put all of your ideas down on paper and not worry about which are "good" or "bad." You will choose the best ideas for your topic in Step 2.

STEP 2: MAKE AN OUTLINE

Complete the outline below with ideas for your paragraph from Step 1.

PARAGRAPH OUTLINE

Topic Sentence	....
Supporting Idea	A. ....
Detail	1. ....
Supporting Idea	B. ....
Detail	1. ....
Supporting Idea	C. ....
Detail	1. ....
Detail	2. ....
Supporting Idea	D. ....
Detail	1. ....
Detail	2. ....
Concluding Sentence	....

STEP 3: WRITE YOUR FIRST DRAFT

Now it is time to write your first draft. Here are some suggestions on how to get started.

1 Use your outline and the sentences you wrote in the Your Turns and in Step 2 above.

2 Focus on making your ideas as clear as possible.

3 Remember to add a title.

After you finish, read your paragraph and check for basic errors.

1 Check that all sentences have subjects and verbs.

2 Go through and look at every comma. Is it correct? Should it be a period?

3 Check that you have used a comma after adverb clauses when they start a sentence.

4 Make sure your topic sentence and supporting sentences are clear.

STEP 4: WRITE YOUR FINAL DRAFT

1 After you receive feedback on your first draft, review it carefully. Fix any errors.

2 Make a note of errors that were most frequent (misspellings, using commas instead of periods, missing verbs). Try to avoid them as you write.

3 Review the Academic Vocabulary and Phrases from this unit. Are there any that you can add to your paragraph?

4 Turn to page 242 and use the Self-Editing Review to check your work.

5 Write your final draft and hand it in.

7 OPINION PARAGRAPHS

GENERAL STUDIES: POPULAR CULTURE

"We all live with the objective of being happy; our lives are all different and yet the same."

Anne Frank
(1929–1945)

About the Author:

Anne Frank was a German-Jewish girl and victim of the Holocaust. She is famous for the diary entries she wrote while she was in hiding.

Work with a partner. Read the quotation about goals. Then answer the questions.

1 An *objective* is a goal. What does the author say is the goal of all people?

2 What other goals do most people share?

3 Do you feel closer to people who share your goals? Why?

Ⓐ Connect to Academic Writing

In this unit, you will learn the skills you need to write your opinion. While some of the writing skills that you will learn may seem new to you, the skill of giving your opinion is not new. In your everyday life, you use opinions to tell people what you like and dislike or what you think about a topic, such as a class or a new food.

Ⓑ Reflect on the Topic

In this section, you will look at a writing prompt and reflect on it. Throughout the unit, you will develop ideas about this prompt. You will use these ideas to practice skills that are necessary to write your paragraph.

The writing prompt below was used for the Student Model paragraph on page 188. The student reflected on the topic and used a concept wheel to brainstorm the best stage of life.

WRITING PROMPT: Some people think our culture is obsessed with being young. What is the best stage of life: childhood, adolescence, adulthood, or old age? Give specific reasons and examples to support your opinion.

ACTIVITY 1.1 Notice

Work with a partner. Discuss at least two more reasons childhood is the best time in a person's life. Share them with the class.

Read the prompt and follow the directions below.

WRITING PROMPT: Should people consider other people's opinions when making choices in life, for example, who to be friends with, what job to have, who to marry? Give specific reasons and examples to support your opinion.

1   Think about your answer. Do you agree or disagree? Write *Agree* or *Disagree* in the center of the wheel.

2   Think about the reasons you feel the way you do. Write them in the wheel.

3   Compare your concept wheel with a partner.

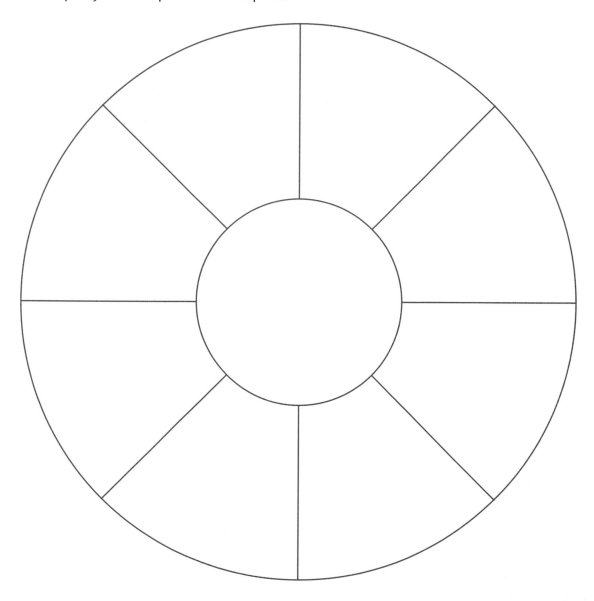

In this section, you will learn academic language that you can use in your opinion paragraph. You will also notice how a professional writer uses this language.

Ⓐ Academic Vocabulary

The words below appear throughout the unit. They are from the Academic Word List or the General Service List. Using these words in your writing will make your ideas clearer and your writing more academic.

adult (n)	illegal (adj)	influence (v)	preference (n)
appreciate (v)	individual (n)	opinion (n)	right (n)

 2.1 Focus on Meaning

Work with a partner. Match the words in bold to their meanings. Write the letters.

A

.... 1 The age when someone becomes an **adult** is different in different countries. In China, the age is 18.

.... 2 I think it should be **illegal** to drive until you are 18. Young people are not safe drivers.

.... 3 Some children do not **appreciate** how hard it is to be a parent.

.... 4 To me, every **individual** under the age of 18 should be able to see any movie they want.

a not allowed by law

b a mature, fully developed person

c a single person or thing

d understand

B

.... 1 All citizens have the **right** to attend local government meetings.

.... 2 A recent survey of teenagers showed a strong **preference** for texting over emailing.

.... 3 Celebrities **influence** what young people wear.

.... 4 In my **opinion**, friends influence children more than parents.

a the legal or moral authority

b a thought or belief about something

c liking one thing more than another

d to affect how something happens

B Academic Collocations

Collocations are words that are frequently used together. Research tells us that the academic vocabulary in Part A is commonly used in the collocations in bold below.

ACTIVITY 2.2 Focus on Meaning

Work with a partner. Read the sentences. Match the collocations in bold to their meanings. Write the letters.

.... 1 My **personal preference** is to always wear a suit to work even though I do not have to.

.... 2 Scientists tell us that a person's diet **directly influences** his or her health.

.... 3 The results in the science experiment showed that people have a **strong preference** for sweet foods.

.... 4 Wei only **expresses her opinion** about the issue to close friends.

.... 5 In the U.S.A., people have a **legal right** to vote in elections.

a something you like more than another thing

b a significant idea of something you like more than another

c affect clearly or without question

d a person's rights protected by a country's laws

e to say what your thought or belief is

C Writing in the Real World

You will read an article titled "The Elderly Rights Law." The author of the article expresses his opinions about this topic.

Before you read, answer this question: What do you think the Elderly Rights Law might be for?

Now read the article. Think about your answers to the question as you read.

The ELDERLY RIGHTS LAW

by Peter Chu

1 Thanks to improvements in health care, people are living much longer lives than in the past. While many continue to be healthy and active in old age, some do not. Because of this, care of the elderly is becoming a top priority. One country where this is particularly true is China.

2 In China, there are over 178 million **adults** 60 or older. By 2030, this number will double. It is no longer common for aging parents to live with their children. Many aging parents do not live with their children as often now as they used to. The relationship between them has changed. The issue of who will care for these elderly **individuals** is a growing concern.

3 Concerned about this problem, the Chinese government created the Elderly Rights Law. The law says that people must look after their parents. It is **illegal** for people to not look after their elderly parents. It doesn't matter how far away they live from each other. Children must visit their parents, and help them financially and emotionally. If children are not dutiful,[1] they may have to pay a fine or go to jail. Is this a good idea?

[1] **dutiful**: doing something because it is expected

4 Some people believe the Elderly Rights Law will help the elderly to live better lives. They believe the law will encourage young people to respect their elders more. Too often, young people do not want to listen to the advice and wisdom of their parents. Also, some people think the law will stop older people from being badly treated. For example, there was a news story about a 91-year-old woman. She was beaten and forced out of her home by her daughter-in-law. The law punishes children for this kind of behavior. Elderly-rights groups point out another benefit of the law. It also addresses the growing problem of loneliness. Many older people are left alone for long periods of time. They get bored and unhappy. Like anyone, they need someone to talk to. Perhaps more importantly, the law emphasizes that young people should think more about the elderly.

5 However, some people are skeptical[2] that the Elderly Rights Law will have any impact. For a start, the law does not say exactly how often a child should visit their elderly parents. Some people also think that visiting family members should be a matter of **personal preference**, not a **legal right**.

6 No one knows if other countries will have a law like China's Elderly Rights Law. Many people agree that something needs to be done about this issue. The elderly population is only going to keep growing. It won't disappear.

[2] **skeptical**: doubtful

 2.3 Check Your Understanding

Discuss the questions below with a partner.

1 What does the Elderly Rights Law make illegal?

2 Why was this law created?

3 Do you think it's a good law? Why or why not?

 2.4 Notice the Features of Opinion Writing

Answer the questions.

1 Read the fourth paragraph. What phrase does the writer use to start this paragraph?

2 How many reasons does the writer give to support the law?

3 Read the fourth and fifth paragraphs. In your opinion, which reasons are the best to support or reject the law?

In Section 1, you saw how the writer of the Student Model reflected on her topic. In this section, you will analyze the final draft of her paragraph. You will learn how to develop ideas for your own paragraph.

Ⓐ Student Model

Read the prompt and answer the questions.

WRITING PROMPT: Some people think our culture is obsessed with being young. What is the best stage of life: childhood, adolescence, adulthood, or old age? Give specific reasons and examples to support your opinion.

1 What is the writing prompt asking the writer to do? Circle the words in the prompt that you expect the writer to use in her paragraph.

2 What are some ideas you think the writer might mention?

Read the paragraph twice. The first time, think about your answers to the questions above. The second time, answer the questions in the Analyze Writing Skills boxes. This will help you notice key features of an opinion paragraph.

STUDENT MODEL

Childhood Is the Best Stage of Life

Many people feel that being an **adult** is the best stage of life, but in my **opinion**, childhood is the best. First, children have more free time than adults because they have school vacations. In my school district, students spend only 180 days in school per year. This means that children have lots of time for fun. For example, they can watch television, play video games, or play outside with friends. Another reason is that children have stronger friendships. This is because children spend more time being with their friends than adults. Adults are often busier and do not have time to be with friends. According to psychologists, the friendships children make often last longer than adult friendships. Third, children have loving family members who **appreciate** them and want to take care of them. For example, families sometimes have parties for childrens' birthdays and other special events, which make these days very happy. Finally, the most important reason is that children do not have to go to work. According to an article I read in the local newspaper, 15% of Americans hate their job. Studying at school is better than working all day, especially in a job you hate. For these reasons, being a child is the most wonderful time of life.

1 Analyze Writing Skills

Underline the words that tell what the writer's opinion is.

2 Analyze Writing Skills

Circle the word that introduces the first reason.

3 Analyze Writing Skills

Underline the phrase the writer uses to give her second reason.

4 Analyze Writing Skills

Underline the words the writer uses to introduce the final reason.

5 Analyze Writing Skills

Circle the phrase the writer uses to introduce the last sentence.

3.1 Check Your Understanding

Answer the questions.

1 What are the four reasons the writer gives to support her opinion?

2 Do you agree that childhood is the best stage of life? Why or why not?

3.2 Outline the Writer's Ideas

Complete the outline for "Childhood Is the Best Stage of Life." Use the phrases in the box.

children are taken care of	spend more time with friends than adults
children do not work	students spend 180 days in school
lots of time for fun	15% of American adults hate their jobs
psychologists: children's friendships are better	

PARAGRAPH OUTLINE

Topic Sentence
Many people feel that being a young adult is the best stage of life, but in my opinion,

childhood is the best.

1st Reason
A. More free time

Supporting Idea
1.

Supporting Idea
2.

2nd Reason
B. Stronger friendships

Supporting Idea
1.

Supporting Idea
2.

3rd Reason
C.

Supporting Idea
1. Happy birthday parties

4th Reason
D.

Supporting Idea
1.

Supporting Idea
2. School better than working all day

Concluding Sentence
Being a child is the most wonderful time of life.

B Opinion Writing

In academic writing, writers often express their **opinions** about ideas and topics. They need to do this in a way that makes the reader really understand their point of view. In order to be convincing, writers need to support their opinions well.

The process of writing an opinion about a topic makes you reflect on the reasons why you feel the way you do. It requires you to analyze your beliefs and support them with your experiences, knowledge of the world, and facts.

An opinion paragraph has the same three parts as all other paragraphs: a topic sentence, supporting sentences and details, and a concluding sentence. In an opinion paragraph,

- the **topic sentence** gives your opinion
- the **supporting sentences** give reasons, facts, explanations, and examples that support your opinion
- the **concluding sentence** restates the topic sentence or summarizes the main idea

In order to write a good opinion paragraph, it is important to understand the difference between a fact and an opinion.

DIFFERENTIATING FACTS AND OPINIONS

Read the sentences below. Which is a fact, and which is an opinion?

The temperature at which water freezes is 32 degrees Fahrenheit.

Where I live, winter is too cold.

The first sentence is a fact. The second sentence is an opinion.

Facts are true. They do not change. The first sentence about the temperature of water freezing is a fact because it is true that the temperature is 32 degrees, and it's not going to change. Facts are statements that experts or scientists agree with. Facts can be found in more than one source. In other words, more than one person knows it is true. Here are some more examples of facts:

In 2007, India produced almost 22 million tons of bananas.

In my neighborhood, there are no supermarkets.

I have two aunts who live in Mexico.

An **opinion**, on the other hand, is what someone believes. People may agree with an opinion or they may disagree with an opinion. For example, people may disagree with the writer about the winter temperatures being too cold. Opinions may or may not be true. Here are some more examples of opinions:

India does not produce enough bananas.

Every neighborhood should have a supermarket.

It would be better for my aunts to move to the U.S.A.

3.3 Identify Facts and Opinions

Write *F* if the statement is a fact. Write *O* if the statement is an opinion.

.... 1 Everyone should quit smoking.

.... 2 Most experts agree that smoking causes cancer.

.... 3 My country, Qatar, is one of the richest countries in the world.

.... 4 In China, there are over 178 million adults 60 or older.

.... 5 Football is more exciting than golf.

.... 6 I live in the state of Missouri.

.... 7 It is wrong to hack into someone else's computer.

 3.4 Apply It to Your Writing

Think about your writing prompt in Section 1 on page 183. Write a fact to support your opinion. Then share your fact with a partner. Ask them to check whether they think what you wrote was a fact or an opinion.

....

....

....

TOPIC SENTENCES IN OPINION WRITING

Good topic sentences clearly respond to the writing prompt. Writers often do this by repeating important words (or related words) from the prompt. They then add their point of view. Writers sometimes use the following words to introduce their opinions.

In my opinion, …

I think (that) …

I believe (that) …

Read the prompts and the topic sentences below. Notice the circled words are repeated in both the prompt and the topic sentence.

1 **WRITING PROMPT:** (Sharing) information about yourself (online) is important to many people's lives. How much sharing is appropriate?

   Topic Sentence: I think that people should not (share) a lot of their private lives (online) for three reasons.

2 **WRITING PROMPT:** Top athletes today receive millions of dollars for playing professional sports. Is their (salary) (appropriate)?

   Topic Sentence: In my opinion, the (salary) top basketball players receive is (appropriate) for several reasons.

3.5 Notice

In the topic sentences at the bottom of page 192, underline the words the writers used to introduce their points of view.

 3.6 Write Topic Sentences

Read each writing prompt below. Underline the words you might repeat in a topic sentence. Then, write a topic sentence for each writing prompt.

1 **WRITING PROMPT:** Some people believe parents are the best teachers. Do you agree or disagree? Use specific reasons and examples to support your opinion.

In my opinion, ...

....

2 **WRITING PROMPT:** Many media sources pay a lot of attention to the lives of celebrities. In your opinion, do the media pay too much attention to public figures? Use specific reasons and examples to support your opinion.

I believe ....

....

....

 3.7 Apply It to Your Writing

Think about your writing prompt in Section 1 on page 183. Write some possible topic sentences. Then share your sentences with a partner. Do you think the sentences clearly respond to the writing prompt? Why or why not?

....

....

....

ADDING REASONS

In the body of an opinion paragraph, writers include **reasons** to support the opinion stated in the topic sentence. It is a good idea to include a few reasons so that the opinion is more convincing.

Each reason usually begins with the following words or phrases:

First, …	*The first reason is …*
Second, …	*Another reason is …*
Third, …	*One more reason is …*
Finally, …	*The most important reason is …*

Complete the paragraph below by adding words or phrases that introduce each reason.

WRITING PROMPT: Top athletes today, such as basketball players, receive millions of dollars for playing professional sports. Is their salary appropriate?

Athlete Salaries Are Appropriate

In my opinion, the salary top basketball players receive is appropriate for several reasons. ...., basketball players work really hard for their money. For example, they have to practice for hours every day, and they play hundreds of games a year. They also have to do dozens of media interviews and publicity events. .... is that top players often only have a short time where they can earn a lot of money. I heard on the radio that the average basketball player's career lasts only four or five years. The .... is that top basketball players inspire others. According to my doctor, children are inspired to stay healthy by watching their favorite sports star. For these reasons, the money top athletes earn is absolutely justified.

3.9 Write Reasons

Complete the topic sentence with your own idea. Then write three reasons to support the topic sentence.

Topic sentence: In my opinion, learning English is ....

1st reason: ....

....

2nd reason: ....

....

3rd reason: ....

....

ADDING SUPPORTING SENTENCES AND DETAILS

These reasons can be supported by more details to make the opinions convincing and clear. Details could include **examples**, **facts**, or **expert opinions**.

Notice how the supporting sentences gave two **examples** of how hard basketball players work. It helps support the writer's opinion. An example could also include a personal story.

REASON   EXAMPLES
First, basketball players work really hard for their money. For example, they have to practice for hours every day, and they play hundreds of games a year. They also have to do dozens of media interviews and publicity events.

Notice below how this supporting sentence uses **a fact**. It helps support the idea that basketball players have short careers.

REASON
Another reason is that top players often only have a short time where they can earn a lot of

FACT
money. I heard on the radio that the average basketball player's career lasts only four or five years.

The supporting sentence below uses the opinions of an **expert** (another person or an official organization) which helps strengthen the writer's argument.

REASON   EXPERT OPINION
The most important reason is that top basketball players inspire others. According to my doctor, children are inspired to stay healthy by watching their favorite sports star.

ACTIVITY **3.10** Add Supporting Sentences

Work with a partner. Add one supporting sentence for each reason below.

1 It is better to be the leader of a group than only a member of a group. First, a leader can
decide what to do. ....

....

....

2 Good parents have many qualities. First of all, good parents have a lot of patience. ....

....

....

ACTIVITY **3.11** Write Supporting Sentences

On a separate piece of paper add a fact, example, or outside source to each of the reasons you wrote for Activity 3.9 on page 195.

ACTIVITY **3.12** Apply It to Your Writing

YOUR TURN

Look at the topic sentences you wrote for Activity 3.7 on page 193. Write a supporting sentence and details for your topic sentence.

....

....

....

....

....

CONCLUDING SENTENCE

The concluding sentence in an opinion paragraph is the same as in the other paragraphs you have studied. It **restates the topic sentence** using different words. Writers do not include any new ideas in the concluding sentence. Writers often start with the following transition phrases:

To conclude, …

For these reasons, …

In sum, …

Look at the topic and concluding sentences below:

<u>Topic sentence</u>: *In my opinion, the salary top basketball players receive is appropriate for several reasons.*

<u>Concluding sentence</u>: *For these reasons, the money top athletes earn is absolutely justified.*

 3.13 Notice

Underline the words or phrases in the concluding statement above that restate the topic sentence.

 3.14 Identify the Sentences

Write TS for the topic sentence, SS for supporting sentences, and CS for the concluding sentence. Then underline the words that helped you determine the answer.

.... 1 Another benefit of globalization is tourism. In 2010, there were over 900 million international tourist arrivals around the world.

.... 2 Finally, globalization has improved the world economy. According to researchers, globalization increases the wealth for poor countries.

.... 3 First, globalization allows for better trade agreements. For example, in the European Union, all 27 member states can trade with each other.

.... 4 For these reasons, I believe globalization has helped people around the world.

.... 5 In my opinion, globalization has benefited many countries.

 3.15 Practice Writing

On a separate piece of paper, write the sentences from Activity 3.14 in order.

Ⓐ Writing Skill 1: Formal vs. Informal Language

It is important to think about your audience when you are writing. Most academic writing uses formal language rather than the language you use when writing to a friend.

USING FORMAL LANGUAGE	
1 Avoid contractions. Note: Some professional writing includes contractions because it makes a sentence "flow" better. Instructors have different rules about using contractions. Ask your instructor what he or she prefers.	*do not* Scientists ~~don't~~ agree on the evidence. *he will* Next year, ~~he'll~~ travel to India.
2 Avoid abbreviations.	*In my opinion,* ~~IMO~~ smoking is a terrible habit. *because* He has a right to speak about this issue ~~b/c~~ it affects him personally.
3 Avoid spoken English.	~~wanna~~ – want to ~~hafta~~ – have to ~~gonna~~ – going to

 4.1 Notice

Find and replace the contractions, abbreviations, and spoken English in the paragraph below. There are five errors.

Adulthood Begins at 18

IMO, adulthood begins at 18 years of age. First, at this age most people are responsible adults. 18-year-olds understand that doing something illegal could mean jail or large fines. This is b/c they know the difference between right and wrong. Second, in many countries, 18-year-olds are old enough to join the military. For example, in my country, Canada, people who wanna join the army can do so at 18. They don't need the consent of their parents. Another reason is that when someone turns 18, they usually don't need their parents for money or a place to live. By this age, most people know that they hafta work and earn money. In conclusion, I believe someone becomes an adult on their 18th birthday.

4.2 Apply It to Your Writing

Look back at your responses to the other Your Turn activities in this unit. Check and correct any informal language you may have used.

Ⓑ Writing Skill 2: Word Forms

Writers often use different forms of a word to add variety and to help make their ideas flow smoothly. When you learn a new word, you can often make new word forms by changing the suffix.

CHANGING WORDS INTO OTHER WORD FORMS	
1 Make nouns by adding one of the following suffixes to verbs: *-tion* *-sion* *-ment*	appreciate → **appreciation** extend → **extension** enjoy → **enjoyment**
2 Make nouns by adding one of the following suffixes to adjectives: *-ness* *-ity*	good → **goodness** normal → **normality**
3 Make adjectives by adding one of the following suffixes to verbs: *-able* *-ible*	achieve → **achievable** access → **accessible**
4 Make adjectives by adding one of the following suffixes to nouns: *-ful* *-y* *-ive*	success → **successful** craze → **crazy** act → **active**
5 Make adverbs by adding *–ly* to adjectives.	different → **differently** preferable → **preferably**

4.3 Change Word Forms

Complete the word form chart. (–) indicates the word does not have that form.
Use a dictionary to help.

NOUN	ADJECTIVE	VERB	ADVERB
		suggest	suggestively
illegality		–	
		inform	
	great	–	
			entertainingly
	related		–
		personalize	

 4.4 Choose Word Forms

Circle the correct word that completes each sentence. Then discuss with a partner what part of speech each correct word is.

Internet Bad for News

I **believer / believe** that the Internet has significantly lowered the quality of news reporting.
(1)
First, there are too many **influence / influential** websites that cover entertainment "news."
(2)
These websites often focus on celebrities' **personal / personally** lives. I do not think this
(3)
information / inform is very important. Second, many websites post
(4)
news items too **quick / quickly** without checking the facts first.
(5)
For example, when a hurricane hit New York **recent / recently**,
(6)
someone posted a photo of a shark swimming down the Hudson
river. It was fake, but many websites, including major news
outlets, showed it. Finally, many news outlets rely on bloggers
and citizen journalists to post stories. Many of these people
are not trained journalists and do not always give a
balanced point of view. In sum, I **strong / strongly**
(7)
feel that the quality of journalism is falling fast
because of the Internet.

C Grammar for Writing: Superlatives

We use the **superlative** to compare and contrast people, places, and things in English. Writers sometimes use superlatives to show a strong opinion.

CREATING SUPERLATIVES

1 For one-syllable adjectives: Add *the* before the adjective. Add -*est* to the end.	*I believe 18 is **the youngest** age a person should be considered an adult.*
Double the final consonant if the adjective ends consonant-vowel-consonant.	*I think Hawaii is **the hottest** state in the United States.*
2 For two-syllable adjectives that end in -*y*: Add *the* before the adjective. Change the -*y* to -*i* and add -*est*.	*Polls suggest that Norway is **the happiest** place on earth.*
3 For other two-syllable adjectives: Add *the most* before the adjective.	*According to scientists, **the most recent** research suggests the world is getting warmer.*
4 For adjectives with three or more syllables: Add *the most* before the adjective.	*I think smoking is **the most dangerous** habit a person can have.*
5 Change *good* to *the best*.	*In my opinion, Harvard is **the best** university.*
6 Change *bad* to *the worst*.	*First, I think that winter is **the worst** time to visit Siberia.*

ACTIVITY 4.5 Write Superlatives

Complete each sentence with the superlative form of the adjectives below. More than one answer is possible.

bad	cheap	healthy	interesting	successful	violent

1 I believe that .... online games are both entertaining and educational.

2 An "F" is .... grade you can get.

3 I think .... essays include up-to-date research.

4 The guide book has information about .... places to stay when on a limited budget.

5 Some researchers think that even .... movies do not make people more likely to be aggressive.

6 Every few months a new report advises people on which foods are .... to eat.

Avoiding Common Mistakes

Research tells us that these are the most common mistakes that students make when using superlatives in academic writing.

1 **Do not use *most* and *-est* with the same adjective.**

   I believe that smoking is the ~~most~~ unhealthiest habit.

2 **Do not use *the most* when you should use *-est*. Do not use *-est* when you should use *the most*.**

   According to some experts, violent movies have made the crime rate the ~~most high~~ highest that they have ever been.

   According to experts, young people are ~~respectfulest~~ the most respectful to older people.

3 **Follow the spelling rules for superlative adjectives.**

   In my opinion, people are the ~~healthyest~~ healthiest and the ~~happyest~~ happiest after they quit smoking.

 4.6 Editing Task

Find and correct five more mistakes in the paragraph below.

College Should Be Free

   In my opinion, college should be free for all students. First, free education is the ~~goodest~~ best way to help the economy in the future. Having the most smartest people will make our country the most competitivest in the world. We would have the bestest doctors, engineers, and teachers. Another reason is because it makes society more equal. Some really talented people, like my friend Asher, cannot go to college because they do not have enough money. Free college means everyone who is accepted can go, no matter how much money they have. This is true in Denmark, which is one of the happyest places to live. Finally, it is wrong to burden people with huge debt at such a young age. According to research, graduates in the U.S.A. have almost $30,000 in loan debt. For some people, it is the expensivest mistake they make. For these reasons, I believe a college education should be free.

D Avoiding Plagiarism

Using quotations is helpful. They help support the ideas in your essay, but it's important to use quotation marks (" ") and the correct punctuation.

My instructor explained that it is acceptable to use the exact words of an expert. However, the writer has to use quotation marks around the words he or she is borrowing to avoid plagiarism. How do I use quotation marks correctly?
– Noora

Dear Noora,

It is worth taking the time to learn the correct way to write a quote. Sometimes you will quote a whole sentence, and other times you will quote just a phrase. Be sure to put those exact words between quotation marks at both the beginning and end of the quote, and follow the rules for punctuating quotations in your writing. Don't forget to mention the author's name, too.

Best,

Professor Wright

USING QUOTATIONS

Quotations are the exact words of an author. When the words are from an expert, they can support your ideas and make them stronger. When you use quotation marks around a quote, it shows that the words belong to someone else and you are just borrowing them.

USING CORRECT PUNCTUATION IN QUOTATIONS

HOW TO QUOTE	EXAMPLES
Introduce the person or source you are quoting	
• Use an introductory phrase such as *according to* [name], or reporting words such as *argue, say, explain, ask*.	***According to*** *Carolyn Foote, "Grades are not everything."*
• Put a comma after the phrase or reporting word.	*Carolyn Foote* ***argues****, "Grades are not everything."*
• Use quotation marks around quote.	
Quote a whole sentence	
• Include the capital letter and punctuation of the original quote inside quotation marks.	*Carolyn Foote says, "**A**nd as policymakers, we can never forget that a test is not the only measure.**"*** *Carolyn Foote asks, "**D**id they have respect for one another's privacy**?**"*
Quote a phrase	
• Use quotation marks around the phrase.	*According to Carolyn Foote, people who work in education* ***"feel like voices crying in the wilderness."***
• Start the quote with a lower case letter, not a capital letter.	
• The period of the whole sentence goes inside the closing quotation mark.	
• Question marks and exclamation points ending the whole sentence go outside the closing quotation mark.	*As Carolyn Foote asks, do teachers want their students to think that* ***"success at any cost is the goal"****?*

 4.7 Practice

Read the paragraph from an original text by Carolyn Foote. Then read the student's sentences. Correct the two punctuation or capitalization errors in each sentence.

Most importantly, we cannot forget that we, as educators, administrators, policymakers, and celebrities, set examples for our children every day. We want every child to succeed. But do we want to show our students that success at any cost is the goal?

1 According to Carolyn Foote, all of us Set examples for our children every day.

2 Carolyn Foote says, "we want every child to succeed".

3 Foote asks "But do we want to show our students that success at any cost is the goal"?

In this section, you will follow the writing process to complete the final draft of your paragraph.

STEP 1: BRAINSTORM
Work with a partner. Follow the steps below to brainstorm more ideas for your topic.

1 First, read the student's brainstorm. She wrote many ideas from the concept wheel she used to reflect on her topic in Section 1 on page 182. Compare the information in her paragraph on page 188 to the concept wheel below. Highlight the ideas that the writer used. Did the writer use all of the ideas in the concept wheel?

STUDENT
MODEL

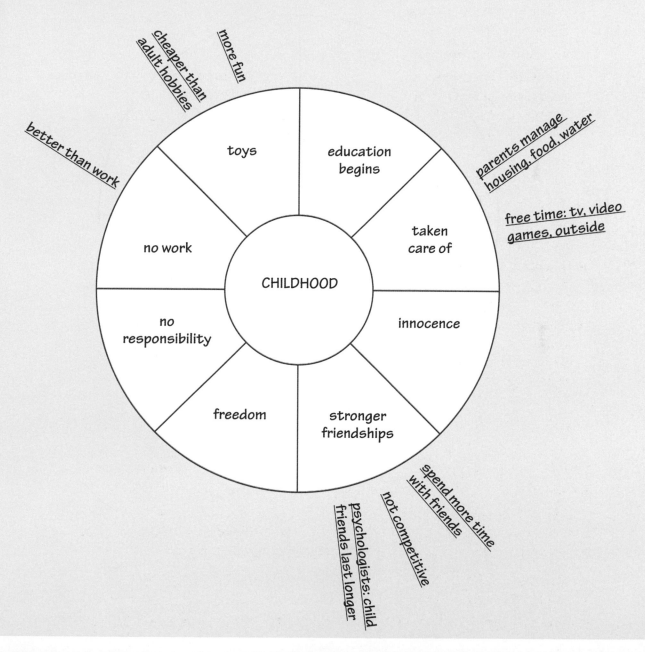

more fun

cheaper than
adult hobbies

better than work

parents manage
housing, food, water

free time: tv, video
games, outside

spend more time
with friends

not competitive

psychologists: child
friends last longer

toys

education
begins

no work

taken
care of

CHILDHOOD

no
responsibility

innocence

freedom

stronger
friendships

2 Now read your writing prompt again. Then review the ideas that you brainstormed in Section 1, page 183. Write the best ones in the concept wheel below. Add ideas from the Your Turns that you completed in the unit. Finally, brainstorm more ideas. You will probably not use every idea, but it is good to write as many ideas as possible.

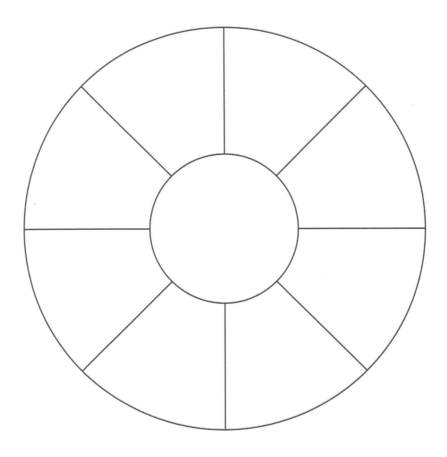

STEP 2: MAKE AN OUTLINE

Complete the outline below with ideas for your paragraph from Step 1.

PARAGRAPH OUTLINE

Topic
Sentence ....

....

1st Reason   A. ....

Supporting
Idea   1. ....

Supporting
Idea   2. ....

Supporting
Idea   3. ....

2nd Reason   B. ....

Supporting
Idea   1. ....

Supporting
Idea   2. ....

Supporting
Idea   3. ....

3rd Reason   C. ....

Supporting
Idea   1. ....

Supporting
Idea   2. ....

Supporting
Idea   3. ....

Concluding
Sentence ....

....

STEP 3: WRITE YOUR FIRST DRAFT

Now it is time to write your first draft. Here are some suggestions on how to get started.

1 Use your outline and the sentences you wrote in the Your Turns and in Step 2 on page 207.

2 Focus on making your ideas as clear as possible.

3 Remember to add facts.

After you finish, read your paragraph and check for basic errors.

1 Check that all sentences have subjects and verbs.

2 Go through and look at every comma. Is it correct? Should it be a period?

3 Check that you have used a comma after adverb clauses when they start a sentence.

4 Make sure your topic sentence and supporting sentences are clear.

STEP 4: WRITE YOUR FINAL DRAFT

1 After you receive feedback on your first draft, review it carefully. Fix any errors.

2 Make a note of errors that were most frequent (misspellings, using commas instead of periods, missing verbs). Try to avoid them as you write.

3 Review the Academic Vocabulary and Academic Collocations from this unit. Are there any that you can add to your paragraph?

4 Turn to page 243 and use the Self-Editing Review to check your work one more time.

5 Write your final draft and hand it in.

8 INTRODUCTION TO ESSAYS

HUMAN RESOURCES: CAREER PATHS

"Don't be afraid to give up the good to go for the great."

John D. Rockefeller
(1839–1937)

About the Author:

John D. Rockefeller was an influential American businessman and cofounder of the Standard Oil Company.

Work with a partner. Read the quotation about work. Then answer the questions.

1 *Go for* means to try to get or accomplish something. What does the author mean by "go for the great?"

2 When in your life have you gone for a great goal instead of a good goal? Were you successful?

Ⓐ Connect to Academic Writing

In this unit, you will learn skills for writing well-organized academic essays. Some of the writing skills you will learn may seem new to you. However, many skills will not be new. When you write an essay, you explain and organize your ideas in a clear way. You use these skills in everyday life, too. For example, you use similar skills to think about reasons to study a certain subject or choose a certain career.

Ⓑ Reflect on the Topic

In this section, you will look at a writing prompt and reflect on it. Throughout the unit, you will develop ideas about this prompt. You will use these ideas to practice skills that are necessary to write your essay.

The writing prompt below was used for the Student Model essay on pages 216–217. The student reflected on his topic and used a cluster diagram to brainstorm ideas about the important values.

WRITING PROMPT: Values are the beliefs, attitudes, and judgments we think are important. Describe the values that are most important in your choice of career. Give specific examples and explanations.

 1.1 Notice

Work with a partner. Look at the cluster diagram. What can you add to the blank circles?

ACTIVITY 1.2 Apply It to Your Writing

Read the prompt and follow the directions below.

WRITING PROMPT: Choose a well-known leader or someone you admire. Write about three values you think this person has. Give examples and explain.

1 Choose one person you would like to write about. Write the person's name in the circle in the middle.

2 Then think about everything you know about this person. What are the values that you admire in this person? Put this information in the other circles. Write short phrases, not sentences. Add more circles if you need them.

3 Compare cluster diagrams with a partner.

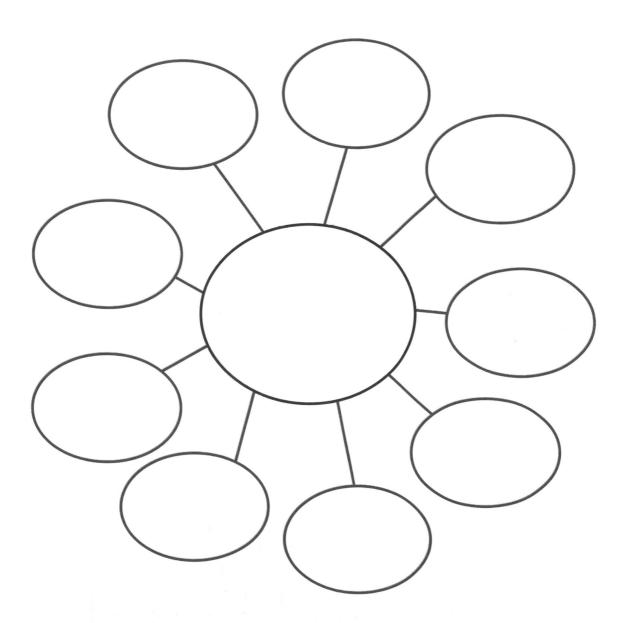

In this section, you will learn academic language that you can use in your essay. You will also notice how a professional writer uses this language.

Ⓐ Academic Vocabulary

The words below appear throughout the unit. They are from the Academic Word List or the General Service List. Using these words in your writing will make your ideas clearer and your writing more academic.

decide (v)	honest (adj)	perform (v)	result (n)
discover (v)	objective (n)	power (n)	security (n)

ACTIVITY 2.1 Focus on Meaning

Work with a partner. Read the sentences. Decide the meaning of the words in bold and circle the correct definitions.

1 The leaders of a country have the **power** to change laws that affect people's lives.
   Power means

   a control or influence.   b knowledge or skill.

2 People like working with him because he's very **honest**. People trust him. **Honest** means

   a rich.   b truthful.

3 Candidates must **perform** different tasks, such as managing projects and writing reports.
   Perform means

   a do an action or piece of work.   b look for or try to find.

4 I do not want to work from 9:00 to 5:00 every day. I'd like a job where I can **decide** my own
   work hours. **Decide** means

   a to have a short work day.   b to choose something.

5 Daniel managed people in his job, but he did not like telling people what to do.
   He **discovered** that he did not like the responsibility. **Discover** means

   a to get a new job.   b to learn or realize.

6 Most actors do not have much job **security**. They are never sure how long a job will last or
   what the next job will be. **Security** means

   a freedom from worry about bad things   b satisfaction or enjoyment of work.
      happening.

7 Susana's **objective** is to become a tour guide when she finishes school. For this reason,
   she is learning languages. **Objective** means

   a a goal.   b an explanation.

8 Some people believe that success comes from good luck. Others say that success is a **result**
   of hard work. **Result** means

   a something that happens because of   b something that happens to lucky people.
      something else, or an effect.

B Academic Phrases

Research tells us that the phrases in bold below are commonly used in academic writing.

> **ACTIVITY** **2.2** Focus on Meaning
>
> **Work with a partner. Match the academic phrases in bold to their meanings. Write the letters.**
>
> .... 1 **In general**, people with careers in showbusiness do not often have much job security.
>
> .... 2 **In particular**, many acting jobs only last a few weeks or months.
>
> .... 3 Also, acting is **a type of** job that requires working unusual hours.
>
> a specifically
>
> b (a) kind of
>
> c typically; in most cases

C Writing in the Real World

You will read an article titled "Which Values? Which Career?" The author of the article organizes her ideas to make them clear to the reader.

Before you read, answer this question: What are *your* personal values?

Now read the article. Think about your answer to the question as you read.

WHICH VALUES? WHICH CAREER?

by Dr. Joan Darcy

1 Are you in a job you hate? Are you deciding which career is right for you? As Confucius (the ancient Chinese philosopher) said: "Choose a job you love, and you will never have to work a day in your life."

2 In general, activities that we love to do never seem like work. Think of famous artists, writers, and scientists with great passion[1] for their work. The **result** of such passion is that they never want to retire. Imagine Pablo Picasso in his studio, working on his art until the day he died at 91! Clearly, he chose the right career for himself.

3 If you know yourself well, you can make a wise career choice, too. How can you "know yourself" better? Career counselors[2] recommend you consider your values when you make decisions about a career.

4 To **discover** your values, read about extrinsic, intrinsic, and lifestyle values below. Then check (✓) whether each value is very important, somewhat important, or not very important to you.

EXTRINSIC VALUES

5 Extrinsic values come from outside a person. They involve the rewards and benefits of a job.

Values	Very important	Somewhat important	Not very important
High pay			
High social position			
Control or **power** on the job			
The ability to travel often			
The ability to work as part of a team			
The ability to **decide** on my own work hours			
A beautiful work environment			
Job **security** and health benefits			

[1] **passion:** powerful emotion, such as love   [2] **counselor:** a person whose job is to give advice

INTRINSIC VALUES

6 Intrinsic values involve a different type of reward. An intrinsic reward brings a person inner[3] satisfaction.[4]

	Very important	Somewhat important	Not very important
Helping other people			
Helping society			
Excitement and adventure[5]			
The ability to influence other people			
Having a sense of achievement			
An opportunity to be creative			
A job that fits with my religious beliefs			
Good relationships with people at work			

LIFESTYLE VALUES

7 Lifestyle values involve where you live and how you spend your time.

	Very important	Somewhat important	Not very important
Having my own home			
Living in a big city			
Living near sports facilities			
Living near theaters, museums, restaurants			
Having time for religion			
Having time to spend with family and friends			
Having fun at work and in life in general			
Having educational opportunities			

8 When you finish, analyze your answers. Which values are very important to you? Are there any surprises? Do they suggest a type of career that might be good for you? Does your career **objective** embrace these values? Let your answers guide you. With this knowledge, you can choose a job where you will "never have to work a day in your life."

[3] **inner**: coming from inside you; private
[4] **satisfaction**: the pleasant feeling you get when you are doing something you want to do
[5] **adventure**: unusual, exciting, and sometimes dangerous experiences

 2.3 Check Your Understanding

Answer the questions with a partner.

1 What does the author tell us about Picasso? Why do you think the author gives this example?

2 What three groups of values does the author list? Why should a person use this checklist?

 2.4 Notice the Features of Essay Writing

Read the first and last paragraphs again. Which words or phrases are similar? Underline them.

In Section 1, you saw how the writer of the Student Model reflected on his topic. In this section, you will analyze the final draft of his essay. You will learn how to develop ideas for your own essay.

Ⓐ Student Model

Read the prompt and answer the questions.

WRITING PROMPT: Values are the beliefs, attitudes, and judgments we think are important. Describe the values that are most important in your choice of career. Give specific examples and explanations.

1 Look at the photo. What do you think a photojournalist does?

2 Read the title. What do you think the writer means when he says photojournalism is "more than just a job"?

Read the essay twice. The first time, think about your answers to the questions above. The second time, answer the questions in the Analyze Writing Skills boxes. This will help you notice the key features of the essay.

Photojournalism: More Than Just a Job

1   Why do some people spend their adult life doing a job they hate? When I was growing up, most of the adults in my life were not happy in their work. In general, they worked only because they needed the salary and health benefits. They wanted job **security**, but they worked all day and were bored. To be **honest**, I never understood this about adults. I **decided** to find a career to make me happy. My **objective** is to become a photojournalist because it is important for me to be creative, have exciting experiences, and learn new things.

> **1 Analyze Writing Skills**
>
> Underline the sentence that tells what the writer will write about. Circle the three reasons that he will discuss.

2   First, being a photojournalist is a creative job. Usually, a photojournalist works with a news reporter to tell a story in a unique way. The reporter uses a notebook or tape recorder and writes the story in words. The photojournalist uses a camera and tells the same story in pictures. Sometimes, a photojournalist works alone and creates a photo essay. A photo essay is a group of pictures about a topic. I like working this way because I can point to the work and say, "I created that!"

3   In addition, the job has excitement and adventure. I will not have to sit at a desk and do the same job eight hours every day. Instead, each day will be different and exciting. This is because I can **perform**

> **2 Analyze Writing Skills**
>
> Underline the topic sentence. Read the last sentence in paragraph 1 again. Circle the word in the topic sentence that the writer uses to connect the ideas to that last sentence.

my job in all sorts of places. For example, I will take photos of famous people who are filming a movie. I will take nature photos of oceans and the animals in them. In particular, I hope to travel around the world and see other cultures.

4   Finally, I want to be a photojournalist because I want to learn new things every day. Each day's job will be a new experience. It will be a daily lesson in how other people think and live. It is a chance to learn about subjects such as music, science, politics, and different religions. I will **discover** things about the world and myself. The **result** is that I can continue to grow and change for my whole life.

5   In conclusion, I want to be a photojournalist because of the creativity, excitement, and opportunity to learn new things. I thought about these values when I **decided** to become a photojournalist. I hope that if I follow these values, I will not spend my life complaining about my work.

> **3 Analyze Writing Skills**
>
> Circle the transitional phrase that the writer uses to show the reader that this will be the last paragraph.

> **4 Analyze Writing Skills**
>
> Read the first sentence and then the last sentence of paragraph 1. The two sentences include the **same / different** ideas.

 3.1 Check Your Understanding

Answer the questions.

1 As a child, what did the writer notice about most adults in his life?

2 How does the writer want his life to be different?

3 What three values are important to the writer?

3.2 Outline the Writer's Ideas

Complete the outline for "Photojournalism: More Than Just a Job." Use the phrases in the box.

reporter uses words, photojournalist uses photos	a creative job
	do job in many different places
music, science, politics	follow these values, not spend my life
adults in my life not happy in their work	complaining about my work

ESSAY OUTLINE

I. Introductory paragraph

Hook Why do some people spend their adult life doing a job they hate?

Background

Thesis Statement My objective is to become a photojournalist because it is important for me to be creative, have exciting experiences, and learn new things.

Body Paragraph 1 II.

Supporting Idea A. Works with a journalist to tell a story

Detail 1.

Detail 2. Photo essays

Body Paragraph 2 III. Excitement/adventure

Supporting Idea A. No need to sit at a desk

Supporting Idea B.

Detail 1. Famous person, nature photos

Body Paragraph 3 IV. Opportunity to learn new things

Supporting Idea A. Subjects

Detail 1.

V. Concluding paragraph

Final Comment

B From Paragraphs to Essays

An essay is a group of paragraphs about one topic. Each paragraph presents a **key point** about the topic and gives more ideas, information, and details. Look at how a paragraph and an essay compare:

PARAGRAPH   **ESSAY**

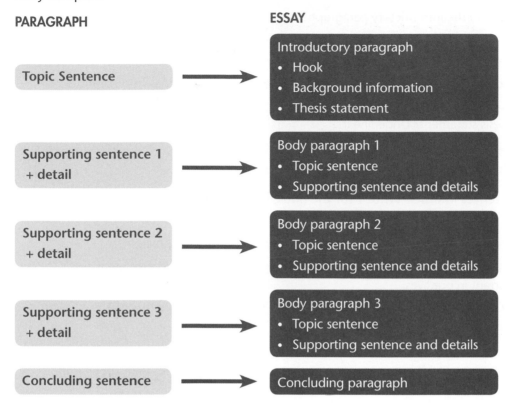

THE INTRODUCTORY PARAGRAPH

The **introductory paragraph** is always the first paragraph of an essay. It includes a **hook**, **background information** about the topic, and a **thesis statement.**

The **hook** is the first sentence in the essay. Its purpose is to grab the reader's attention. The hook could be:

- a famous quotation or saying,
- an interesting fact, or
- a question. The question is usually answered in the introductory or concluding paragraph.

After the hook, a writer often includes a few sentences of **background information.** These sentences help readers understand the topic. Background information can be:

- general information about the topic,
- a story that helps readers understand why the topic is important, or
- historical information.

The **thesis statement** is the last sentence in the introductory paragraph and tells the reader what the essay is about. It is similar to a topic sentence for a paragraph. It includes the topic and the writer's **point of view** (similar to the controlling idea in a paragraph). The thesis statement contains the topics that the body paragraphs will discuss.

3.3 Identify the Parts

Read the introductory paragraph of the Student Model essay again on pages 216–217. Answer the questions.

1 What is the hook in the introductory paragraph? Underline it.

2 What type of hook is it: quotation, fact, or question?

3 What is the background information in the introductory paragraph? Circle it.

4 What type of background information is it: general information, a personal story, or historical information?

5 What is the thesis statement? Underline it.

 3.4 Choose the Order of Sentences in an Introduction

A Put these sentences in order. Write 1 for the hook, 2–5 for background information, and 6 for the thesis statement.

.... a However, good workplace relationships can make us much happier.

.... b Because we spend so much time with them, people in the workplace are very important in our lives.

.... c Sixty percent means that these people spend more time at work than with friends or family.

.... d Most people spend 60% of their life working.

.... e For a happier life, it is important to encourage good relationships with supervisors, co-workers, and employees.

.... f Poor relationships at work can cause stress and unhappiness in life in general.

B Write the sentences from Part A in paragraph form on a separate piece of paper.

WRITING GOOD THESIS STATEMENTS

The **thesis statement** is the most important sentence in an essay. When people read the thesis statement, they know what to expect in the rest of the essay. A good thesis statement:

• answers the writing prompt

• gives the topic

• gives the writer's point of view

The thesis statement also often gives **aspects,** or parts, of the writer's point of view. These aspects give the reader a "map," or plan, of the rest of the essay. Each of the aspects introduces one of the body paragraphs, *in the same order.*

Look at the thesis statement below from the Student Model. The three aspects are underlined.

My objective is to become a photojournalist because it is important for me to <u>be creative</u>, <u>have exciting experiences</u>, and <u>learn new things</u>.

In the Student Model, the writer introduces the topic sentence of each body paragraph using each aspect in the thesis statement:

Aspect 1: *be creative*

Topic sentence in body paragraph 1: *Being a photojournalist is a creative job.*

Aspect 2: *have exciting experiences*

Topic sentence in body paragraph 2: *The job has excitement and adventure.*

Aspect 3: *learn new things*

Topic sentence in body paragraph 3: *Finally, I want to be a photojournalist because I want to learn new things every day.*

 3.5 Recognize Good Thesis Statements

Work with another student. Read the prompt and thesis statements below. Which do you think are good thesis statements? Which are not good? Why not? Check (✓) the appropriate boxes.

WRITING PROMPT: People work because they need money to live. In your opinion, what are some other reasons that people work? Use specific examples to support your opinion.

1 Thesis statement: *In my opinion, people work because they need money for themselves, their family, and their future.*

☐ Good

☐ Not good

☐ If not good, why? It does not _____

2 Thesis statement: *I believe people work to feel self-respect, meet other people, and have a sense of achievement.*

☐ Good

☐ Not good

☐ If not good, why? It does not _____

3 Thesis statement: *I think people work because it gives them a sense of purpose and lets them feel needed.*

☐ Good

☐ Not good

☐ If not good, why? It does not _____

3.6 Write Thesis Statements

Read the topic sentences below. For each group of three topic sentences, write one good thesis statement.

1 **WRITING PROMPT**: What does success mean to you? How will you know that you are a success?

   Topic sentence 1: I will feel that I am a success when I have control over my own schedule.

   Topic sentence 2: I will know that I am successful when I own my own business.

   Topic sentence 3: Another sign of success will be when I have a sense of achievement.

   Thesis statement: ....

   ....

2 **WRITING PROMPT**: In your opinion, why is money important? Give three reasons and support them with specific information and examples.

   Topic sentence 1: Money is important because it provides us with the basic needs in life.

   Topic sentence 2: Another reason money is important is that it allows us to support our family members.

   Topic sentence 3: We also need money because it lets us help other people in society.

   Thesis statement: ....

   ....

3 **WRITING PROMPT**: In your opinion, how should people spend their free time? Give three ways and support them with specific information.

   Topic sentence 1: It is essential to exercise in your free time.

   Topic sentence 2: Another important way to spend free time is by becoming a better person.

   Topic sentence 3: Also, it is important to spend time on relationships with friends and family.

   Thesis statement: ....

   ....

3.7 Apply It to Your Writing

YOUR TURN

Use the cluster diagram that you created in Section 1 on page 211. Choose three of the values. Then write a thesis statement with three parts in your controlling idea. Share this sentence with a partner.

....

....

....

THE BODY PARAGRAPHS

The **body paragraphs** in an essay have regular paragraph structure: a topic sentence, supporting sentences, and details such as reasons and examples. They may also have a concluding sentence. Each body paragraph relates to one aspect of the thesis statement.

Writers sometimes, but not always, use the following transition words and phrases to introduce each body paragraph:

> *First,*
>
> *In addition,*
>
> *Finally,*

 3.8 Notice

Look at body paragraph 3 in the Student Model essay again on pages 216–217.
Then, answer the questions.

1 Write the topic sentence. Underline the transition word.

....

....

....

2 Write the supporting sentences the writer uses to support the topic sentence.

....

....

....

3 Write the reason he gives why each day will be different and exciting.

....

....

....

4 Write one of the examples the writer gives.

....

....

....

A Choose the correct topic sentences for each body paragraph below. Write the number.

1 Another reason money is important is that it allows us to support our family members.

2 We also need money because it lets us help other people in society.

3 Money is important because it provides us with the basic needs in life.

Body Paragraph A

.... The most basic need, of course, is food. Without food, there is no life. Thousands of years ago, people hunted for meat and walked around looking for fruits and nuts. Today, we have supermarkets, but money is necessary to buy the food there. The next basic need is a type of shelter. We need a place to live, a house or apartment. Money is necessary for rent or house payments. The third basic need is clothing. We must cover our bodies and protect them from cold or hot weather. Some people spend huge amounts of money on designer clothes. This is not necessary, but money is necessary for even simple clothes.

Body Paragraph B

.... Without money, we cannot provide the basic needs for our family. However, we always want to give family members more than just the basic needs. If we have children, we want them to have a good education. In some countries, school is not free. Parents must pay school fees. In places with free public education, there are still expenses. For example, children might need to buy books, uniforms, or materials for class projects. We want a good life, in general, for all family members. Money is necessary for this. In particular, we need money for birthday gifts, summer vacations, or a movie on Saturday night.

Body Paragraph C

.... We are all members of society. This carries with it a responsibility. We must help people who cannot help themselves. One way to do this is with money. In particular, money can buy food for food banks. It can help a poor family pay doctors bills they cannot afford. It can help people who do not have a home. Sometimes, a small amount of money can make a big change in someone else's life.

B Choose one of the paragraphs above. Underline the supporting sentences. Double underline the details.

 3.10 Apply It to Your Writing

Use the thesis statement you wrote in Activity 3.7 on page 222. Write three topic sentences based on this thesis statement. Make sure they are in the same order as the three parts of your controlling idea. Then share your sentences with a partner.

....

....

....

....

THE CONCLUDING PARAGRAPH

The concluding paragraph in an essay **restates the thesis statement** from the introductory paragraph. It should include the aspects from the thesis statement in the same order. For example:

Thesis statement in the introduction:

My objective is to become an engineer because it is important for me to solve problems, learn new things, and work hard.

Restated thesis statement in the conclusion:

Problem-solving, an opportunity to learn, and hard work are values I considered in my goal to become an engineer.

In the example above, the writer made these changes to restate the thesis:

- a change of order: In the introduction, the main idea (*become a engineer*) was first and the controlling idea next. In the conclusion, he used the opposite order.

- a change of words (synonyms) without a change of meaning: He changed *objective*, in the introduction, to *goal* in the conclusion.

- a change of parts of speech: The writer changed the verb phrases (*solve problems, learn new things, and work hard*) to nouns or noun phrases (*Problem-solving, an opportunity to learn, and hard work*).

A concluding paragraph can include a **final comment**. This comment might be a suggestion or recommendation about something that people should do. It can be one or more sentences. For example:

For these reasons, I think it is important to base a career choice on our values.

The comment may refer back to something in the introduction. For example:

Introduction:

When I was growing up, most of the adults in my life … <u>complained about their jobs</u>.

Comment in the conclusion:

I hope that if I follow these values, <u>I will not spend my life complaining about my work</u>.

If the hook in the introduction was a question, the comment can answer this question in one or two sentences.

In the concluding paragraph, avoid adding new information to the essay. Also, do not include sentences such as "This is the end of my essay" or "We are at the end of the essay." The reader understands that the conclusion is the end of the essay.

3.11 Restate the Thesis Statement

Each sentence below is a thesis statement from the introduction of an essay. Restate it for the concluding paragraph. Compare your sentences with a partner.

1 Thesis statement: *I hope to become an animator because I love to draw pictures, make people laugh, and have fun.*

   Restatement: ....

   ....

   ....

2 Thesis statement: *An airline pilot must be responsible, calm, and intelligent.*

   Restatement: ....

   ....

   ....

3 Thesis statement: *A good hairdresser is a creative person, a good listener, and a positive thinker.*

   Restatement: ....

   ....

   ....

 3.12 Make a Comment

Read this introduction and concluding paragraph. Choose the best comment to end the conclusion. Write the letter.

Introduction:

    There is a saying that "Money is the root of all evil." This means that money is a bad thing. Maybe it is bad if people are greedy and want too much money. However, I think an important value in life is having enough money. Money is important because it provides us with basic needs, allows us to support our family, and makes it possible to help others in society.

Concluding paragraph:

    To conclude, without money we cannot cover our basic needs, take care of our family, or help others in the society.

....

....

a That is all there is to say about the issue of money being good and not bad.

b In the modern world, money is necessary. It is not "the root of all evil." It is important to have the right attitude about money.

c Money is also important because we can use it to make our lives more interesting and exciting. For example, paying to see a movie or a concert.

Ⓐ Writing Skill: Avoiding Run-on Sentences and Comma Splices

Two common types of mistakes with sentence structure are **run-on sentences** and **comma splices**.

A **run-on sentence** (or **run-on**) is two sentences – independent clauses – incorrectly connected without punctuation or conjunctions. For example:

I enjoy my job it is fun.

A **comma splice** is two or more sentences incorrectly connected by a comma instead of a period. For example:

I enjoy my job, it is fun.

CORRECTING RUN-ONS AND COMMA SPLICES	
1 Separate the sentences. Put a period after the first sentence. Begin the second sentence with a capital letter.	*I enjoy my job. It is fun.*
2 Use a subordinating conjunction (see Unit 3) such as *because, when, if, before,* and *after.*	*I enjoy my job because it is fun.*
3 Use a coordinating conjunction (see Unit 5) such as *and, but, so,* and *or.*	*I enjoy my job, and it is fun.*

 4.1 Identify and Correct Run-ons and Comma Splices

A Read these body paragraphs from a student's essay. Find run-ons and comma splices. Circle the places where two sentences incorrectly come together.

A good nanny must be very patient children do things that can make adults crazy. Some babies cry for hours. At the age of two, a child's favorite word is "no." Children can also get very angry they throw themselves on the floor and cry. Some children ask a lot of questions. Some children want the nanny to read the same story to them over and over. Many adults do not have the patience for this, a good nanny has a lot of patience.

A good nanny must also be a creative thinker. A nanny needs to create activities that children like. Children enjoy surprises, they like to discover things. Also, it is essential for a nanny to think of ways to solve problems, the nanny is often alone all day with the children. The parents are not there to give directions the nanny must take responsibility for things that go wrong.

The third characteristic of a good nanny is the ability to multitask. In a home with several children, many things happen at the same time. The nanny must be able to cook dinner for older children with one hand with another hand she feeds the baby. With her third hand, she helps a child with homework, with her fourth hand, she plays a game with another child. As you see, it is necessary for a nanny to have many hands.

B Now correct the mistakes you found in Part A above. Rewrite the paragraphs on a separate sheet of paper.

ⓑ Grammar for Writing: Parallel Structure

Parallel structure is helpful for writing clear thesis statements and supporting sentences in your essay. You need parallel structure when your sentence has two or more items in a list, such as the three aspects of the thesis statement.

PARALLEL STRUCTURE	
For parallel structure, all items in a list should use the same part of speech. Each item also should be a similar length. For example: • noun (or noun phrase), noun (or noun phrase), and noun (or noun phrase) • verb (or verb phrase), verb (or verb phrase), and verb (or verb phrase) • adjective, adjective, and adjective	*A good nanny must have <u>patience</u>, <u>creativity</u>, and <u>the ability to multitask</u>.* *Money is important because it <u>provides us with basic needs</u>, <u>allows us to support our family</u>, and <u>makes it possible to help others in society</u>.* *To discover your own values, use this checklist of <u>extrinsic</u>, <u>intrinsic</u>, and <u>lifestyle</u> values.*

 4.2 Use Parallel Structure in Supporting Sentences

In each sentence below, one item is not parallel. Delete or add words so that all the items are the same part of speech.

1 A nanny cooks dinner, feeds the baby, is a helper with homework, and plays games.

2 The world is very different from 100 years ago because of advances in technology, education, and better healthcare.

3 It is a chance to learn about subjects such as music, science, politics, and how people think about religion.

4 Happiness comes from achievement and being creative.

5 My work environment is enjoyable, fun, and has friendly co-workers.

Avoiding Common Mistakes

Research tells us that these are the most common mistakes that students make when using parallel structure in academic writing.

---

1 Do not mix the parts of speech in a list.

In his free time, Jeremy enjoys dinner with friends and ~~to go hiking~~ ^hikes^ in the mountains.

Lorena's new job pays well, offers educational opportunities, and ~~fun~~ ^allows for fun^.

2 Make each item in a list the same or similar in length.

In his free time, Jeremy enjoys dinner with friends ~~at his own home because he is a fabulous cook~~ and hikes in the mountains.

Lorena's new job pays well, offers educational opportunities ~~at the company or at a local college~~, and allows for fun.

 4.3 Editing Task

Find and correct two more mistakes in the paragraph below.

Choosing a Career

In the past, most people had no opportunity to choose their own career. They did the same work as their parents, were hired as apprentices, or ~~the landowner gave them work~~ ^were given work by the landowner^ If a father was a farmer, the son had to stay and farm, too. If the king picked someone for his army, the person became a soldier. Most women had to stay home. They had to cook meals, clean clothes by hand in a sink in the kitchen, and care for children. Today, most people can choose whatever career they want. I feel fortunate to live in a time when I can follow my passion for computers, mathematics, and learn about the universe.

C Avoiding Plagiarism

Writing an academic paper takes planning, organization, and research.

I'm learning how to write academic papers. My instructor mentioned that in the future we would write essays. We would do research and include the researched ideas in our essays. She said we would list the sources of those ideas under "Works Cited." What's a "Work Cited"?
– Tenley

Dear Tenley,

"Works Cited" is a list of all your sources. It is the last page of your essay. It is usually written in a specific format. There are a variety of formats you can use. In this book, you will use the MLA style. Find out the format your instructor wants for your paper. Take careful notes on each source while you do your research. It will make it easier to write your Works Cited page later.

Best,

Professor Wright

CREATING A "WORKS CITED" PAGE

At the end of each essay, you will add a Works Cited page. This page includes all the sources used for the essay. The sources are listed alphabetically by the author's last name. The name is followed by specific information in a very precise style. When you write a citation, you must pay attention to these three things:

- complete information (author, title, publisher, city of publication, date of publication, page, print or online)
- order of information
- punctuation (including quotation marks) and *italics*

CITING SOURCES USING THE MLA FORMAT

1 Books

| AUTHOR'S LAST NAME | FIRST NAME | | TITLE | | CITY OF PUBLICATION | PUBLISHER |

Greene, Howard. *College Grad Seeks Future*. New York: St. Martin's,

| YEAR OF PUBLICATION | MEDIUM |

2010. Print.

2 Magazine articles

| AUTHOR'S LAST NAME | FIRST NAME | TITLE OF ARTICLE | TITLE OF MAGAZINE | DAY | MONTH | YEAR |

Webber, Rebecca. "Reinvent Yourself." *Psychology Today* 06 May 2014:

| PAGES | MEDIUM OF PUBLICATION |

23–26. Print.

3 Newspaper articles

| AUTHOR'S LAST NAME | FIRST NAME | TITLE OF ARTICLE |

Woods, Randy. "Ready to Change Careers? Think Like a Millennial."

| NEWSPAPER | DAY | MONTH | YEAR | PAGE | MEDIUM |

Seattle Times 20 July 2014: F1. Print.

4 Articles from the Web

| AUTHOR'S LAST NAME | FIRST NAME | TITLE OF ARTICLE |

Townsley, Debra. "Preparing Students for Careers of Tomorrow."

| TITLE OF WEBSITE | PUBLISHER OF WEBSITE | DAY | MONTH | YEAR | MEDIUM | DATE YOU READ THE ARTICLE |

Huffington Post. Huffington Post, 9 Sept. 2012. Web. 4 Aug. 2014.

4.4 Practice

A Read the citations. Is everything in the correct order? If not, circle the items that are not in the right order. Write it in the correct order.

1 Book
Ritsert Jansen. *Funding Your Career in Science*. 2013. New York: Cambridge, Print.

2 Magazine
Warner, Judith. *New York Times Magazine*. Print. "The Opt-Out Generation Wants Back In."
7 Aug. 2013: 34–38.

3 Web article
"Coping with a Career Crisis." Chronicle of Higher Education, Sternberg, Robert. 27 Jan.
2014. *Chronicle of Higher Education*. Web. 15 Sept. 2014.

5 WRITE YOUR ESSAY

In this section, you will follow the writing process to complete the final draft of your essay.

STEP 1: BRAINSTORM

Work with a partner. Follow the steps below to brainstorm more ideas for your topic.

1 Before you start, notice how the writer of the Student Model changed his cluster diagram. Compare the information in his cluster diagram on page 210 to the cluster diagram below and answer the questions:

   a Why do you think he re-organized his ideas in this way?

   b Highlight the ideas that the writer thought were the most important.

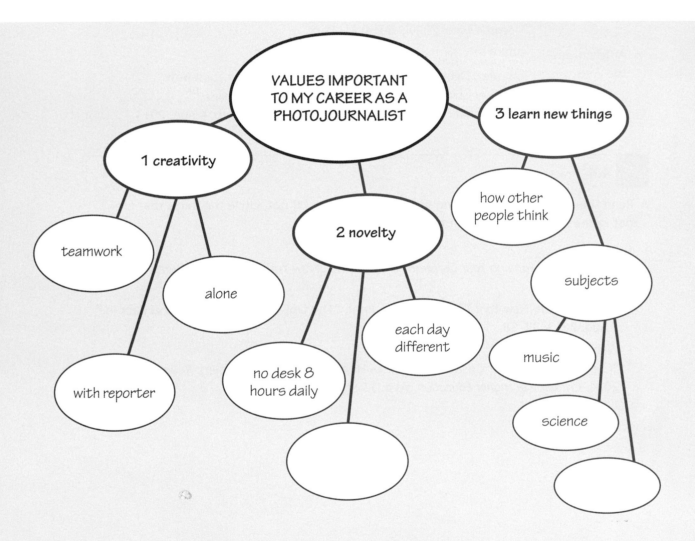

2 Now start your brainstorm. First think of people you know and all the values that you can think of. Then, choose a person and three values you have the most ideas about. Add them to the cluster diagram below.

3 Brainstorm supporting ideas (for example, explanations or your own personal experiences) and write those in the circles extending from the value circle. Add more circles if you need to. Use ideas from the Your Turns you completed.

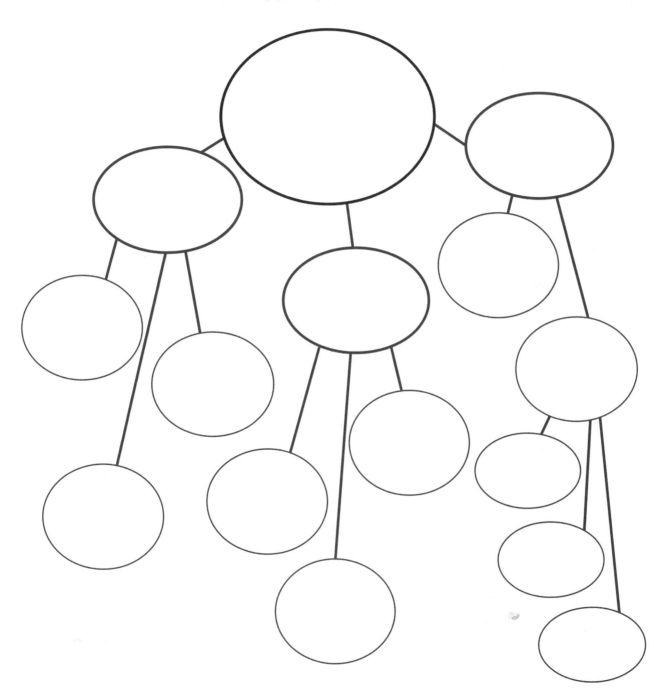

STEP 2: MAKE AN OUTLINE

Complete the outline below with your ideas from the previous steps. Include the ideas that you wrote in the Your Turn activities throughout the unit.

ESSAY OUTLINE

Introductory paragraph	I.
Hook	
Thesis Statement	
Body Paragraph 1: 1st Value	II.
Supporting Idea	A.
Detail	1.
Detail	2.
Supporting Idea	B.
Detail	1.
Detail	2.
Body Paragraph 2: 2nd Value	III.
Supporting Idea	A.
Detail	1.
Detail	2.
Supporting Idea	B.
Detail	1.
Detail	2.

Body Paragraph 3: 3rd Value	IV. ....
Supporting Idea	A. ....
Detail	1. ....
Detail	2. ....
Supporting Idea	B. ....
Detail	1. ....
Detail	2. ....
Concluding Paragraph	V. ....
Concluding Sentence	....
	....

STEP 3: WRITE YOUR FIRST DRAFT

Now it is time to write your first draft. Here are some suggestions on how to get started.

1 Use your outline and the sentences you wrote in the Your Turns and in Step 2 above.

2 Decide on a good hook to begin your introductory paragraph. If this hook is a question, remember to answer it in the introduction or conclusion.

3 Add a comment in your concluding paragraph.

4 Remember to add a title.

After you finish, read your paragraph and check for basic errors.

1 Check that all sentences have subjects and verbs.

2 Go through and look at every comma. Is it correct? Should it be a period?

3 Check that you have used a comma after adverb clauses when they start a sentence.

4 Make sure your topic sentence and supporting sentences are clear.

STEP 4: WRITE YOUR FINAL DRAFT

1 After you receive feedback on your first draft, review it carefully. Fix any errors.

2 Make a note of errors that were most frequent (misspellings, using commas instead of periods, missing verbs). Try to avoid them as you write.

3 Review the Academic Vocabulary and Phrases from this unit. Are there any that you can add to your essay?

4 Turn to page 244 and use the Self-Editing Review to check your work.

5 Write your final draft and hand it in.

SELF-EDITING REVIEW

1 DEVELOPING IDEAS
TECHNOLOGY: COMMUNICATING IN THE MODERN WORLD

Self-Editing: Review Your Work	Completed
1 Check your paragraph one last time. Include examples, reasons, and explanations. Make sure you use correct signal words.	
2 Make sure your paragraph includes both simple sentences and compound sentences.	
3 Use capital letters correctly.	
4 Use punctuation correctly.	
5 Underline the Academic Vocabulary words and Academic Collocations you used. Make sure you used at least two academic words and one collocation.	
6 Underline all simple present verbs and make sure you avoided any mistakes.	
7 Review any feedback and think about mistakes that you typically make, such as using the wrong simple present forms or putting adverbs of frequency in the wrong place. Make a list of your common mistakes here: .... Look for these mistakes in your writing and correct them.	

Self-Editing: Review Your Work	Completed
1 Check your paragraph one last time. Include a topic sentence, three supporting sentences, specific details, and a concluding sentence.	
2 Organize your ideas by ranking and using language such as *first, second,* and *third*.	
3 Use capital letters and punctuation correctly.	
4 Add a title.	
5 Underline the Academic Vocabulary words and phrases and verb + preposition combinations you used. Make sure you used at least two words and one collocation.	
6 Review any feedback and think about mistakes that you typically make, such as using the wrong verb tense or form of the verb, using commas instead of periods, missing "a/an" and "the." Make a list of your common mistakes here.	

Look for these mistakes in your writing and correct them.

Self-Editing: Review Your Work	Completed
1 Check your paragraph one last time. Include examples of phrases describing the chronological order of events.	
2 Make sure your paragraph includes both simple sentences and complex sentences.	
3 Use capital letters correctly.	
4 Use punctuation correctly.	
5 Add a title.	
6 Underline the Academic Vocabulary words and Academic Collocations you used. Make sure you used at least two academic words and one collocation.	
7 Underline all pronouns and make sure you avoided any mistakes.	
8 Review any feedback and think about mistakes that you typically make, such as using the wrong simple present forms or putting adverbs of frequency in the wrong place. Make a list of your common mistakes here. .... Look for these mistakes in your writing and correct them.	

Self-Editing: Review Your Work	Completed

1 Check your paragraph one last time. Are all of the steps in the correct order?

2 Make sure your paragraph includes transitions for sequential ordering.

3 Check the details after the steps. Do they add support?

4 Include at least one reminder or warning.

5 Add a title.

6 Underline the Academic Vocabulary words and phrases you used. Make sure you used at least one academic phrase.

7 Circle all the imperative forms and make sure you avoided any mistakes.

8 Review any feedback and think about mistakes that you typically make, such as using the wrong imperative form, or not using *Do not* correctly. Make a list of your common mistakes here.

....

....

....

Look for these mistakes in your writing and correct them.

Self-Editing: Review Your Work	Completed
1 Check your paragraph one last time. Does the topic sentence contain a simple definition?	
2 Make sure your paragraph includes supporting details that help explain the definition.	
3 Are all the details relevant? Is there any irrelevant information?	
4 Circle all the coordinating conjunctions. Are they used correctly, with correct punctuation?	
5 Add a title.	
6 Underline the Academic Vocabulary words and Academic Collocations you used. Make sure you used at least two words and one collocation.	
7 Underline all the subject relative clauses, and make sure you avoided any mistakes.	
8 Review any feedback and think about mistakes that you typically make, such as using the wrong relative pronoun, or including a subject pronoun after a relative pronoun. Make a list of your common mistakes here.	

....

....

....

Look for these mistakes in your writing and correct them.

Self-Editing: Review Your Work	Completed
1 Check your paragraph one last time. Do you have a topic sentence with a controlling idea?	
2 Did you choose one type of spatial organization (such as clockwise or most important part first)?	
3 Do you have at least two supporting sentences?	
4 Does each supporting sentence have at least one detail?	
5 Do you have correct use of *there is / there are*?	
6 Does your paragraph have adjectives and adverbs to make your description richer?	
7 Underline the Academic Vocabulary words and phrases you used. Make sure you used at least two words and one phrase.	
8 Add a title.	
9 Review any feedback and think about mistakes that you typically make, such as using *there is / there are* incorrectly or not including details. Make a list of your common mistakes here.	

....

....

....

Look for these mistakes in your writing and correct them.

Self-Editing: Review Your Work	Completed
1 Check your paragraph one last time. Did you include a topic sentence, three reasons, specific facts, examples, and experiences, and a concluding sentence?	
2 Organize your ideas by using key words and phrases to introduce facts and opinions and reasons.	
3 Use capital letters and punctuation correctly.	
4 Add a title.	
5 Underline the Academic Vocabulary words and Academic Collocations you used. Make sure you used at least two words and one superlative.	
6 Review any feedback and think about mistakes that you typically make, such as using the wrong verb tense or form of the verb, using commas instead of periods, missing "a/an" and "the." Make a list of your common mistakes here.	

....

....

....

Look for these mistakes in your writing and correct them.

Self-Editing: Review Your Work	Completed
1 Check your essay one last time. Do you have a thesis statement with three aspects in the controlling idea?	
2 Does the thesis statement have parallel structure?	
3 Does each body paragraph have a topic sentence that comes from the thesis statement?	
4 Are the three topic sentences in the same order as the three aspects of the thesis statement?	
5 Do you have at least two supporting sentences in each body paragraph?	
6 Does each supporting sentence have at least one detail?	
7 Is your sentence structure correct (no run-ons or comma splices)?	
8 Is the concluding statement in the same order as the thesis statement?	
9 Does the concluding statement have different words from the thesis statement?	
10 Underline the Academic Vocabulary words and phrases you used. Make sure you used at least two words and one phrase.	
11 Add a title.	
12 Review any feedback and think about mistakes that you typically make, such as with run-ons or comma splices. Make a list of your common mistakes here.	

....

....

....

Look for these mistakes in your writing and correct them.

SOURCES

The following sources were consulted during the development of Final Draft *Student's Book 1.*

Unit 1

Duggan, Maeve, and Lee Rainie. "Cell Phone Activities 2012." *Pew Research Center*. Pew Research Center, 25 Nov. 2012. Web. 18 May 2015.

Quan, Kristene. "Nepal Says Historic Everest Video Call Was Illegal." *Time*. Time, 22 May 2013. Web. 18 May 2015.

Unit 2

Brown, Joel. "Why It Is Important to Fail." Success Advice. *Addicted2Success*. Addicted2Success, n.d. Web. 18 May 2015.

"Felix Baumgartner and Team Celebrate Supersonic Freefall Anniversary." *Space.com*. Purch, n.d. Web. Video. 18 May 2015.

"Felix Baumgartner Pilot Biography." *Red Bull Stratos*. Red Bull Air Race, n.d. Web. 18 May 2015.

"50 Famously Successful People Who Failed at First." *OnlineCollege.org*. Online Colleges, 16 Feb. 2010. Web. 18 May 2015.

"Innovative Minds Unite to Overcome Engineering Challenges in One of the Most Hostile Environments Known to Man." *Red Bull Stratos*. Red Bull Air Race, n.d. Web. 18 May 2015.

Red Bull. "Felix Baumgartner's Supersonic Freefall from 128k'—Mission Highlights." *YouTube*. YouTube, 14 Oct. 2012. Web. Video. 18 May 2015.

"Robert Pershing Wadlow." *Alton Museum of History and Art*. Alton Web, n.d. Web. 18 May 2015.

"Robert Wadlow—8 Feet 11.1 Inches (272 cm)." *TheTallestMan.com*. TheTallestMan.com, n.d. Web. 18 May 2015.

Scott, Nate. "Felix Baumgartner Jumped from the Stratosphere and Would Like to Talk about Anything Else." *USA Today*. Gannett/USA Today Sports Digital, 4 Apr. 2014. Web. 18 May 2015.

"Tallest Man Ever." *Guinness World Records*. Guinness World Records, n.d. Web. 18 May 2015.

Tierney, John. "24 Miles, 4 Minutes and 834 M.P.H., All in One Jump." *New York Times*. New York Times, 14 Oct. 2012. Web.

Unit 3

Ryan, Megan. "Reaction to the Salk Polio Vaccine Clinical Trials." *The Albert B. Sabin Digitization Project*. University of Cincinnati Libraries' Blog (LiBlog), 14 Mar. 2012. Web. 18 May 2015.

"Salk Produces Polio Vaccine 1952." People and Discoveries. *PBS*. WGBH, n.d. Web. 18 May 2015.

"Sleep." Common College Heath Issues. *Health Promotion*. Brown University, n.d. Web. 18 May 2015.

Unit 4

Stampler, Laura. "The Incredible Story of Karen Kaplan's Meteoric Rise from Receptionist to CEO." *Business Insider*. Business Insider, 29 May 2013. Web. 18 May 2015.

Ward, Alexandra. "Receptionist to CEO: Karen Kaplan Did It at Ad Agency Hill Holliday." *Newsmax*. Newsmax Media, 30 May 2013. Web. 18 May 2015.

Unit 5

Adams, Susan. "It Still Pays to Get a College Degree." *Forbes*. Forbes. 10 Jan. 2013. Web. 18 May 2015.

"The Benefits of Earning a College Degree." *College Atlas*. CollegeAtlas.org, n.d. Web. 18 May 2015.

Di Maria, David L. "Plagiarism from a Cross-Cultural Perspective." *Al Jamiat*. Al Jamiat Magazine, 4 June 2009. Web. 18 May 2015.

Huffington, Arianna. "Redefining Success: The Third Metric." *Graduation Wisdom*. Graduation Wisdom, May 2013. Web. 18 May. 2015.

McGuire, Jeff. "The Benefits of Having a College Education." Articles and Advice. *CollegeView*. Hobsons, n.d. Web. 18 May 2015.

Wann, Lizzie. "Why Your College Degree Has More Value Than You Think." Brazen Life. *Huffington Post*. Huffington Post, 2 June 2013. Web. 18 May 2015.

Unit 6

Alexander, Caroline. "If the Stones Could Speak: Searching for the Meaning of Stonehenge." *National Geographic*. National Geographic Society, June 2008. Web. 18 May 2015.

Bennett, Karen. "The Geopolitics of Academic Plagiarism." *Academia.edu*. Academia, n.d. Web. 18 May 2015.

"Cultural Perspective on Plagiarism." *WSU Libraries*. Washington State University, n.d. Web. 18 May 2015.

Donohue, Christiane. "When Copying Is Not Copying: Plagiarism and French Composition Scholarship." *Originality, Imitation, and Plagiarism: Teaching Writing in the Digital Age*. Ed. Caroline Eisner and Martha Vicinus. Ann Arbor: U of Michigan, 2008. 90–103. Print.

"Flag of Malaysia." *Wikipedia*. Wikipedia, n.d. Web. 18 May 2015.

"Great Buddha of Kamakura." *Sacred Destinations*. Sacred Destinations, n.d. Web. 18 May 2015.

"Great Pyramid of Giza." *Wikipedia*. Wikipedia, n.d. Web. 18 May 2015.

"Leaning Tower of Pisa." *Wikipedia*. Wikipedia, n.d. Web. 18 May 2015.

"Leaning Tower of Pisa Facts." Engineering Facts. *Science Kids*. Science Kids, n.d. Web. 18 May 2015.

Mattingly-Arthur, Megan. "Leaning Tower of Pisa History." *eHow*. Demand Media, n.d. Web. 18 May 2015.

Mitchell, Sam. "Morocco Souks and Markets." *Morocco Travel Guide—Journey Beyond Travel*. Journey Beyond Travel. n.d. Web. 18 May 2015.

"Mount Rushmore." *Wikipedia*. Wikipedia, n.d. Web. 18 May 2015.

"Oval Office." *Wikipedia*. Wikipedia, n.d. Web. 18 May 2015.

Renoir, Pierre-Auguste. *Luncheon of the Boating Party*. 1880–1881. *Phillips Collection*. Phillips Collection, n.d. Web. 18 May 2015.

"Saint Basil's Cathedral." *Wikipedia*. Wikipedia, n.d. Web. 18 May 2015.

"Saint Basil's Cathedral in Moscow." *Famous Wonders*. Famouswonders.com, n.d. Web. 18 May 2015.

"Souq." *Wikipedia*. Wikipedia, n.d. Web. 18 May 2015.

"Statue of Liberty." *Wikipedia*. Wikipedia, n.d. Web. 18 May 2015.

"St. Basil's Cathedral." *Moscow.Info*. Moscow.Info, n.d. Web. 18 May 2015.

Stemwedel, Janet D. "Cultural Differences of Opinion about Plagiarism." Adventures in Ethics and Science. *ScienceBlogs*. ScienceBlogs, 9 Oct. 2006. Web. 18 May 2015.

"Stonehenge." *Wikipedia*. Wikipedia, n.d. Web. 18 May 2015.

"Taj Mahal." *Wikipedia*. Wikipedia, n.d. Web. 18 May 2015.

Unit 7

Bennington, Emily. "Should College Be Free?" *Huffington Post*. Huffington Post, 25 May 2011. Web. 18 May 2015.

Castillo, Michelle. "China Law Brings Attention to Pros, Cons of Caring for Aging Parent." *CBS News*. CBS Interactive, 1 July 2013. Web. 18 May 2015.

Ellis, Blake. "Average Student Loan Debt: $29,400." *CNN Money*. Cable News Network, 5 Dec. 2013. Web. 18 May 2015.

Foote, Carolyn. "More Than a Test Score." *Huffington Post*. Huffington Post, 14 Oct. 2010. Web. 18 May 2015.

Hatton, Celia. "New China Law Says Children 'Must Visit Parents.'" *BBC News*. BBC, 1 July 2013. Web. 18 May 2015.

Martinez-Carter, Karina. "How the Elderly Are Treated around the World." *The Week*. The Week, 23 July 2013. Web. 18 May 2015.

Singh, Sukhdeep S. "Why College Education Should Be Free for Everyone." *EzineArticles.com*. SparkNET 15 Apr. 2011. Web. 18 May 2015.

Unit 8

Boer, Pat. "Work Values Checklist." *Monster.com*. Monster, n.d. Web. 18 May 2015.

"Do You Know the Basics?" Work. *Manifest Your Potential*. C. A. Dowler, n.d. Web. 18 May 2015.

INDEX

Words that are part of the Academic Word List are noted with an Ⓐ in this index.

ART CREDITS

The authors and publishers acknowledge the following sources of copyright material and are grateful for the permissions granted. While every effort has been made, it has not always been possible to identify the sources of all the material used, or to trace all copyright holders. If any omissions are brought to our notice, we will be happy to include the appropriate acknowledgements on reprinting and in the next update to the digital edition, as applicable.

The publishers are grateful to the following for permission to reproduce copyright photographs and material:

T = Top, B = Below, L = Left, R = Right, C = Centre, B/G = Background

p. 3: Alex Belomlinsky/Getty (1), Andy Whale/Getty (2), Brian A Jackson/Shutterstock (3), Matthias Breiter/Getty (4), BsWei/Getty (5), Neil Webb/Getty (6), Diogo Salles/Getty (7), lvcandy/Getty (8), p. 6: Keystone-France/Gamma-Keystone/Getty, p. 7: sculpies/Shutterstock (TL), Fulcanelli/Shutterstock (TC), alfredolon/Shutterstock (TR), emran/Shutterstock (BL), p. 8: Nerthuz/Shutterstock, p. 9: Keystone-France/Gamma-Keystone/Getty, p. 13: Alex Belomlinsky/Getty, p. 18: Lighthunter/Shutterstock, p. 21: Justin Lewis/Getty, p. 24: Amble Design/Shutterstock, p. 28: andresr/Getty, p. 35: Cliff Hide News/Alamy, p. 36: saaton/Shutterstock, p. 37: Amble Design/Shutterstock, p. 43: Andy Whale/Getty, p. 47: Keystone-France/Gamma-Keystone/Getty, p. 49: EDB Image Archive/Alamy, p. 50: wavebreakmedia/Shutterstock, p. 56: svetikd/Getty, p. 60: lapon pinta/Shutterstock, p. 63: Bettmann/Corbis, p. 65: AE Pictures Inc./Getty, p. 68: lukas_zb/Shutterstock, p. 73: Brian A Jackson/Shutterstock, p. 77: Shahril KHMD/Shutterstock, p. 78: baranq/Shutterstock, p. 80: stockcreations/Shutterstock, p. 83: AlexSutula/Shutterstock, p. 85: Alan Dawson Photography/Alamy, p. 90: bhofack2/Getty, p. 92: Everett Collection Historical/Alamy, p. 95: Ron Fehling/Masterfile/Corbis, p. 96: Tetra Images/Alamy, p. 101: Matthias Breiter/Getty, p. 105: Randy Faris/Corbis, p. 106: Karen Kaplan/Hill Holliday, p. 109: Zero Creatives/Getty, p. 116: imageBROKER/Alamy, p. 122: Vstock/Alamy, p. 123: sunabesyou/Shutterstock, p. 129: BsWei/Getty, p. 135: Dan Dalton/Getty, p. 137: Juice Images/Alamy, p. 145: Ammentorp Photography/Shutterstock, p. 149: Nerthuz/Shutterstock, p. 150: Piotr Marcinski/Shutterstock, p. 155: Neil Webb/Getty, p. 159: Mark Schwettmann/Shutterstock, p. 160: sculpies/Shutterstock (L), p. 160: Fulcanelli/Shutterstock (R), p. 161: alfredolon/Shutterstock, p. 162: emran/Shutterstock, p. 167: Leks052/Shutterstock, p. 170: Joseph Sohm/Shutterstock, p. 172: Pornsak Paewlumfaek/Shutterstock, p. 176: naka-stockphoto/Shutterstock, p. 181: Diogo Salles/Getty, p. 186: Inmagineasia/Getty, p. 189: Sergey Novikov/Shutterstock, p. 194: ZUMA Press, Inc/Alamy, p. 198: wragg/Getty, p. 200: OJO_Images/Getty, p. 202: Pgiam/Getty, p. 203: PathDoc/Shutterstock, p. 209: lvcandy/Getty, p. 213: Steve Debenport/Getty, p. 214: Geber86/Getty, p. 217: Semmick Photo/Shutterstock, p. 230: Daniel M Ernst/Shutterstock

Author images courtesy of Cambridge University Press p. 10: Jeanne Lambert (T), David Bohlke (TC), Robyn Brinks (BC), Pamela Hartmann (B)

Cover image: danielsbfoto/Getty

CORPUS

Development of this publication has made use of the Cambridge English Corpus (CEC). The CEC is a multi-billion word computer database of contemporary spoken and written English. It includes British English, American English and other varieties of English. It also includes the Cambridge Learner Corpus, developed in collaboration with the University of Cambridge ESOL Examinations. Cambridge University Press has built up the CEC to provide evidence about language use that helps to produce better language teaching materials.

NOTES

NOTES

NOTES